Understanding

Circumcision

in the Bible

and

Its Meaning for

Christian Families

Today

By

Samuel Martin

STUDIES IN GENESIS SERIES

Volume Three

This volume is dedicated to my late father Dr. Ernest L. Martin (1932-2002)

The New
Foundation
for
Biblical
Research
Jerusalem

Table of Contents

Introduction:
Understanding Circumcision in the Bible
and Its Meaning for Christian Families Today

Every year in Israel around the middle of November, there is a feast and pilgrimage that Christians make to the St. George Church in Lydda (modern Lod). Christians from every corner of Israel (and beyond) attend this feast. The feast lasts for several days with people coming to the grave of St. George to offer their prayers and thanks for his intercession to God on their behalf. Some of the Christian communities who live fairly near to the church (within five or six miles) come walking to the church on foot to remember the suffering of St George, who died as a martyr in 303 AD.

I have visited this pilgrimage many times and spoken to many of the people attending the pilgrimage. They come because they attribute to St. George many miracles in their lives and come to pay their vows, give their gifts and acknowledge the importance of this saint in their lives and in the works he has wrought to help them. People bring large plastic tans full of freshly pressed olive oil to anoint St. George's grave to then be collected and sent around the world.

Men and women tell stories of miraculous healings. People tell stories of vows they have made and prayers that have been answered which they attribute to the intercession of St. George. Women who were never able to have children bring their sons and daughters as witnesses to the miracles wrought through St. George. Boys born during the feast are called George. Seemingly every mother or father in attendance is "Imm George" (the mother of George) or "Abu George" (the father of George).

When you attend this holiday, it is a happy time, a time of miracles, it is a time of thanksgiving, it is a time of love and smiling faces. It is a time of sharing the story of St. George with one's children and the importance of the saint in our lives as a bringer of miracles and a call to a holier life. Little children and babies are brought to the church to be blessed and anointed with oil from St. George's grave. It is a time to remember dark times of pain concerning the martyrdom of St. George, but where our miraculous God stepped in and changed history. It is a time where babies born are celebrated, cherished, loved and remembered.

While St. George is no longer with us, this feast is alive and well and the people who believe in his intercessory role in our lives are carrying on his message of Christ. This feast is a celebration of St. George's life (and remembering his very traumatic death) and how he and his life continue to touch the followers of our Lord Jesus Christ today.

Now, let us go back in time, back to a time 4,000 years ago. We are still in the land of Israel (when it was called Canaan) and now we are going to talk about other feasts and celebrations. It was also a festive time around the time of the winter solstice (which takes place between December 20-23 depending on the year). People were assembling for the feast. They were preparing to make their vows and getting ready for the annual sacrifice. Food was being prepared and people were wishing their neighbors well.

Different groups were participating in the feast in honor of different gods. This was almost 500 years before Moses lived and many different gods were worshipped. The anticipation was high for the culmination of the feast and the day of the sacrifice, because instead of celebrating life, these dear people were going to celebrate death, the death of their own children! That is right! These people celebrating this feast were going to sacrifice their own children to these different gods. People whose children died were to be congratulated and the event of their child being killed was going to be celebrated!

The same thing was happening in Egypt in the springtime before the rains. This is because during the annual prayers and festivals undertaken before the Nile river rose and provided the water needed for the farmers living near it, one young girl was chosen to be offered as a human sacrifice by drowning to the god who, as the people then believed, provided the rains that allowed the river to rise enough to meet the needs of the people at that time. Another celebration of death. This annual sacrifice continued every year only ending almost 1,500 years ago.

Into this world of darkness, the LORD, the maker of heaven and earth and the true God who is the exponent of Love and Light, saw that it was time to change the behavior of mankind. To do this, the LORD chose to give a new teaching to the patriarch Abraham and that teaching was circumcision. God, who is Love, decided to act out of love for His children. This teaching was destined to change the world at that time and bring about a revolution in thinking in a world dominated by darkness and death to move people towards light and life. It is this truth that we are going to study in this book.

The Focus of This Book: Circumcision in the United States of America

Circumcision is a religious practice, which is widespread today. In the USA, it is estimated that between 500,000 and 1,000,000 circumcisions take place annually.[1] It represents a very important decision that many American Christian families will make concerning their baby boys. Because the author of this book is an American, this book is directed to Christians mainly in the USA who are still taking part in ritual infant circumcision in the tens of thousands each year. More understanding is needed now on this subject than ever before.

---

[1] Dr. Ryan McAllister - http://keepyoursonsintact.weebly.com/1/post/2014/03/the-nonethics-of-routine-infant-circumcision1.html

Since I became a theological activist against the corporal punishment of children in 1994 (spanking/smacking), and through the subsequent publication of my book *"Thy Rod and Thy Staff, They Comfort Me; Christians and the Spanking Controversy"* in 2006, I have noticed that the dynamics surrounding the issues of spanking/smacking/corporal punishment and circumcision are very similar among Christian families. What I have learned is that often some Christian mothers face a personal situation of individual and collective anguish over the issue of circumcision before, during and after giving birth to their boy babies.

Because my book dealing with the subject of spanking/smacking/corporal punishment was so popular with Christian mothers, this fact allowed me to develop a close connection with scores of Christian mothers who were able to give me a great deal of personal feedback and information. Over the years, the subject of circumcision would come up periodically so slowly I began to seek more information about this subject because it was one which caused great concern and often very major consternation mainly for Christian mothers.

One of my close online American friends (a mother of three children) commented in 2016 how she personally regretted the decision to circumcise both of her sons. Even at the time she did it, she did not really feel right about undertaking the procedure. Additionally, when circumcision comes up in online discussions that I have seen, the subject seems to spiral out of control so fast with people taking the pro or con of the argument and some people shaming those who had their sons circumcised. Some online forums and Facebook groups that I have seen are just really quick to stop comments because this can be such a heated issue to discuss. People hold very passionate views on this most controversial subject, but it seems few really understand or have studied carefully the biblical teachings behind it. I know from my own experience with this issue that my level of understanding on this subject was also very limited. That all changed when I began to research this subject in greater detail.

More and more I have seen a horrible tension that exists with Christian mothers in particular over this issue. I have even heard from one mother that she prayed not to have a son because she did not want to face this issue. The problem that I see coming up over and over again is that husbands, who are themselves circumcised, take very strong opinions and often force their wives to circumcise their sons often against their own wishes and intuitive feelings. In addition, families also pressure young mothers to undertake the procedure and young mothers often get talked into doing something that they don't want to do. Strong pressures often also come from parents and in laws and other relatives. The consternation that takes place on this issue in families is staggering and it is not an isolated issue. It affects tens of thousands of Christian families every year.

This is a very confusing issue for Christians overall and Christian mothers in particular. Christian dads are less confused because they normally want their sons to look like them physically and over the last several generations in the USA in particular, circumcision has become a very commonly done medical procedure.

What I have often found is that most Christians are fairly clear about the Biblical teachings surrounding circumcision for the Christian and that for non-Jewish believers, there is direct teaching in the New Testament showing that circumcision is no longer mandatory for Christians,[2] although I have seen some use certain Bible texts to point out that the practice may still be relevant for Christians today. However, the problem that Christian mothers face often has nothing to do with what the Bible teaches, but rather it concerns culture, tradition and prevailing practices in many families that often isolates them and forces them against their maternal intuitions and wills to have their sons circumcised.

---

[2] Acts 15; Galatians 5:2

Many Christian mothers face this issue hearing arguments and assertions from their husbands and other family members telling them that circumcision and circumcised men are more "hygienic"[3] or "healthier" than uncircumcised men or that a father wants his son to be "like dad" or perhaps other men in the family.

In addition to family pressures, parents may also face medical opinions from medical professionals in favor of circumcision. Definitely, the opinions of medical professionals are given serious weight by families in such decisions and this can add to an already stressful environment for undertaking this very sensitive and important medical decision.

To add to the whole matter, one has to understand that surgical procedures are individual to the person receiving them. While I am not a medical doctor, it is obvious to me that no two surgeries are the same exactly. One licensed and trained surgeon that I know very well told me directly that it is known that some surgeons who do circumcisions do them in a "horrible" way and there is really no accountability for families to change the result because once it is done, it is pretty much done and hard to undo or repair without major expense.

I was also told that while circumcision according to the Bible is supposed to take place on the eighth day of life, circumcision often takes place as early as day two in some American medical settings and in fact this timeline interferes with breast-feeding. This is because on the first day of life, babies are normally very tired. On the second day, babies start to wake up more and to feed more and this feeding helps bring in more mature mother's milk. So, if a child is circumcised on day two of life, then due to the operation, babies remain sleepy and this means that proper milk flow from the mother can be interrupted or not proceed from the mother during these early days when the baby needs mother's milk the most, according to God's design.

---

[3] https://matthewtontonoz.com/2015/01/05/why-is-circumcision-so-popular-in-america/

I am aware of a case of someone that I know directly who was circumcised by a physician and the end result was not what was hoped for. This matter, which became known within a particular religious denomination, affected the decisions of other parents who refused to use that doctor again because of the "botched circumcision." The tragedy of such a situation is hard for most people to fathom.

I guess for me seeing the pain this issue causes, the confusion and consternation and psychological isolation it can bring to Christian mothers, the inflexibility of some Christian men and other relatives who force Christian mothers to "obey" and have this elective procedure done (and the potential sadly that children could be harmed from this procedure) has caused me to carefully study the whole matter of circumcision with a view to educating Christians.

It can be so confusing for pregnant mothers who are soon to give birth to face all of these pressures which often go against their maternal intuition. Of course, in the Christian environment today, this becomes crazy making for mothers because then they are faced with the issue of going against the wishes of their husbands and all of the baggage and supposed biblical teaching which is put forward for moms to get them to do what their husbands and their families want.

This fact I found so disturbing and painful that a mother, who is experiencing such a beautiful thing as a blessed family addition would have to deal with such painful psychological feelings. In addition, when a young mother (or a mother of any age) feels totally alone in this feeling, it must be horrible to have to go through such an experience. It is difficult enough going through pregnancy and all of the emotions that experience brings to have to add to it these horrible psychological issues surrounding circumcision, what I have seen is that for some Christian mothers, the feelings are so strong they are almost unbearable. So many Christian mothers feel strongly about this issue, but they face overwhelming opposition from their husbands or even their own families who demand that their sons be circumcised. This leads to situations of terrible isolation during a time when any kind of negative feelings should be nowhere near a pregnant mother.

Writing about the subject of circumcision in the Christian context is not easy

Circumcision is not an easy subject to write about for me. It involves a very sensitive and important religious practice to the faith of Judaism, a faith that I love and respect deeply. I grew up in a Sabbatarian Christian Church keeping the Sabbath and Holy Days.[4] My focus, however, on this issue targets only Christians who are struggling with a decision to circumcise or are seeking more accurate Bible knowledge about the subject of circumcision what it meant in ancient times.

What I can say though is that in my limited experience with circumcision among Jewish believers is that the tensions and issues that exist with Christian mothers are generally speaking not found in the same way with Jewish believers. It is a simple fact that within Judaism, circumcision of males is an absolute religious requirement. There is no choice in the matter (unless there is a known medical issue which could delay performing the circumcision until a later time). The whole culture around circumcision is generally positive (as far as I know) and that it is considered one of the most holy events in the life of a family. Circumcision is an event of great joy and happiness.

This is, however, for Christians not the case. Circumcision in a Christian family involves a specific choice. Christian parents are required to give a specific permission to a medical authority to circumcise their sons. The environment in a Christian context surrounding the matter of circumcision is fundamentally

---

[4] I was raised in the World Wide Church of God, a Christian church that was Sabbath and Holy Day keeping and followed most of the calendrical and kosher laws found in Judaism.

different than that which is present within Judaism. Because of this difference and the fact that a choice is involved, this is where great tension exists on a personal level with Christian mothers mostly bearing the greatest burden over this matter.

My position on circumcision in the Christian context

I am not in favor of circumcision for Christians other than some urgent medical diagnosis from a qualified medical authority saying that the procedure must be performed due to some life-threatening medical necessity. (I cannot imagine what that might be as I am not a doctor) The reason I do not favor the procedure is the New Testament injunction against it coupled with the very real risk in any surgical procedure that something, God forbid, could go wrong.

What This Research Is Trying to Achieve

I have several goals in publishing this research. First, I want to provide solid biblical evidence to help Christians have accurate, thorough information on circumcision and what the Bible teaches us about it and what it meant in the past. Second, I also want to provide Christian families facing the choice of circumcision with a solid academic tool to help them in engaging with stakeholders concerning their decision making surrounding the subject of circumcision. We really need to have more biblical understanding on this issue to help all make better decisions.

In conclusion, circumcision is a biblical teaching, which is not so easy to understand, but when you do understand it in the right way, you will find that it represented an important teaching that the LORD gave to mankind some 4,000 years ago for their benefit. Having said that, we Christians understand that God has changed this requirement for believers in Jesus Christ as their Messiah.

1. Circumcision: What it was and wasn't in Ancient Times

To begin, we need to define exactly what we are talking about when we are speaking about circumcision. This is because there appears to be some teachings about this issue and some interpretations about the practice in ancient times compared to what it is today. Here, I would like to refer to authoritative scholarly references to help us better define what circumcision is.

"Circumcision (Hebrew *milah*; sometimes *berit milah* "covenant of circumcision": Ceremony of cutting away the foreskin practiced by many peoples including the Semites."[5]

"In its characteristic form the operation of circumcision consists in drawing forward the prepuce (with proper precautions, as by a shield, to prevent any incision of the *glans*), which, when sufficiently protracted, is amputated …"[6]

"Circumcision (מולה, *mulah*'; Septuagint and New Testament περιτομή, which is translated by the Latin *circumcisio*, i.e., a *cutting around*), a custom among many Eastern nations of cutting off part of the prepuce, as a religious ceremony."[7]

It seems fairly clear that what we are talking about is the removal of the foreskin in a surgical procedure which has not changed a lot since ancient times.

In general, I believe we can know that the foreskin was removed and cut off because we have ancient records which point to the practice of a surgical

---

[5] Roth, The Standard Jewish Encyclopedia: Doubleday and Company, Inc.: Garden City, New York, 1959. Pg. 446.
[6] Hastings, Encyclopedia of Religion and Ethics: T & T Clark; New York, 1910. Pg. 659
[7] McLintock and Strongs, Cyclopedia of Biblical, Theological and Ecclesiastical Literature: Harper and Brothers, New York, 1883. Vol. II, Pg. 347.

14

procedure being provided to some people (that is people who had been circumcised), who wished to reverse the procedure so that they appeared like other uncircumcised males. Note the following references:

"Jewish hellenists, wanting to assimilate to the Greek way of life, underwent operations to obliterate the sign of circumcision."[8]

"Some of the Jews in the time of Antiochus Epiphanes (2nd Century BCE), wishing to assimilate themselves to the heathen around them, built a gymnasium at Jerusalem, and, that they might not be known to be Jews when they appeared naked in the games, 'made themselves uncircumcised'.[9] Sometimes this was done with a surgical operation such as Celsus describes[10], sometimes by other means. (Dioscor. 4:157) The term for this was ἐπισπασθαι (Talm. משך ערלה), i.e. *drawing over again*, se. the prepuce.[11] Against having recourse to this practice from an excessive anti-Judaistic tendency, the apostle Paul cautions the Corinthians in the words, "Was anyone called being circumcised, let him not become uncircumcised." (μὴ ἐπισπάσθω, I Corinthians 7:18)"[12]

Therefore, we see a description of what circumcision entailed and how some people who had been circumcised in ancient times, for a variety of reasons, sought to have the procedure reversed.

---

[8] Roth, The Standard Jewish Encyclopedia: Doubleday and Company, Inc.: Garden City, New York, 1959. pg. 446.

[9] See note 6 - (I Maccabees 1:15 ἐποίησαν ἑαυτοῖς ἀκροβυστίας; Lat. Vulgate *fecerunt sibi preputia*; Josephus Antiquities 12:5.1

[10] See Note 6 - (De Medic, 7:25; compare Galen, *Meth. Med.* 14:16; Paul *AEgin* 6:53; Epiphanius, *De pond. et mens.* P. 538, ed. Basil, 1544)

[11] See Note 6 - (4 Maccabees 7; see Batholin, *Morb. bibl.* 26)

[12] McLintock and Strongs, Cyclopedia of Biblical, Theological and Ecclesiastical Literature: Harper and Brothers, New York, 1883. Pg. 350.

Some have put forward the idea that circumcision may have not involved a process of complete foreskin amputation as it is today undertaken[13], but rather a procedure involving just cutting the prepuce in some way short of full amputation or only removing a very small portion of the prepuce. The Bible, though, seems clear (along with quite a lot of other supporting sources that we have referred to here) that in circumcision, the entire foreskin was indeed removed.[14]

There is a lot of debate concerning this issue of how much of the foreskin was removed. Whatever the case may be, anyone who suggests that all or part of the foreskin was not removed will need to take this rather graphic passage of Scripture into consideration in their analysis:

"Then Saul said, "Thus shall you say to David, 'The king desires no marriage present except a hundred foreskins of the Philistines, that he may be avenged on the king's enemies.'" Now Saul planned to make David fall by the hand of the Philistines. When his servants told David these words, David was well pleased to be the king's son-in-law. Before the time had expired, David rose and went, along with his men, and killed one hundred of the Philistines; and David brought their foreskins, which were given in full number to the king, that he might become the king's son-in-law. Saul gave him his daughter Michal as a wife." (I Samuel 18:25-27 NRSV)

---

[13] "According to the anthropologist and sociologist Nissan Rubin, the Jewish form of circumcision, called brit mila, during the first two millennia did not include the later customary periah, namely the complete scraping of the inner foreskin from the glans. This was only added around 135 AD, to make it impossible to restore the foreskin by stretching, which became popular in the wake of Hellenic influence. While originally only the tip of the foreskin was cut off, periah removes the entire foreskin." - https://en.intactiwiki.org/index.php/Circumcision
[14] Exodus 4:25; I Samuel 18:27

(Comment: I would like to assert regardless of whether the entire foreskin was removed or not, **what is most important is that the spiritual meaning, reasoning and rationale for undertaking circumcision in the first place remains the same**. In addition, whether a part or all of the foreskin was removed, both procedures were an operation which would alter the physical appearance of the individual who was having the procedure. Therefore, the person would appear physically different than others in an external physical sense.)

The late Dr. Ernest L. Martin in discussing circumcision points out a key symbolic meaning: "circumcision was that a part of their flesh had died. This was a symbol as the apostle Paul later stated in his epistles that God's people have "died" to the world -- especially that carnal part that is detrimental to us and to the rest of society."[15] This interpretation would make no sense if a part of the foreskin remained attached to the body in a physical sense because it would remain alive.

To conclude, in this study, we assert circumcision today means the whole foreskin is removed.

---

[15] Dr. Ernest L. Martin, June Communicator: ASK: Portland, OR:1991

2. Circumcision: A sign among other signs mentioned in the Bible

Circumcision is linked to the Hebrew word *ohth* (אות). This word is translated by various English words in the Authorized Version including: sign, mark, token, ensign, miracle.

This word in this context means that it is a visible sign understood to show:

"a sign of the binding relationship between the Jew and God."[16]

We encounter this word the first time in the Bible connected to a human being with the person of Cain, who received a "mark" (Hebrew word *ohth* אות) after he killed his brother Abel.[17] This was something visibly external to Cain and had a specific meaning.

Rabbi Chill (*ibid.*) points out that there are several other signs "*ohthot*" (plural of *ohth*) mentioned in the Bible such as:

- The Sabbath (Exodus 31:13)
- The Wearing of Phylacteries (Deuteronomy 6:8)

These signs had meanings associated with them. Note the explanation from CBTEL:

---

[16] Chill, The Mitzvot: The Commandments & their Rationale: Keter Books: Jerusalem,1974, 377
[17] For more information on this subject, see my work "What was the Mark of Cain?" – Available here https://www.amazon.com/gp/product/B08ZVNBT54/ref=dbs_a_def_rwt_bibl_vppi_i0

"In Biblical language a sign is a token, or whatever serves to express or represent another thing. Thus, the LORD gave to Noah the rainbow as a sign of his covenant (Gen.9:12,13), and for the same purpose he appointed circumcision to Abraham (Genesis 17:11, see Exodus 3:12; Judges 6:17).[18]

When it comes to circumcision, it is important for us to understand what this sign or token really expresses or represents. This question will be the focus for the remainder of this book.

---

[18] CBTEL, Vol. IX, pg. 735

3. The modern ceremony of Circumcision and its link to the ancient rite

In studying the practice of circumcision, it is good as much as possible to really understand what is taking place during this ritual. Make no mistake about it; there is much to be learned about what is really taking place during the circumcision and what the ritual really means to those taking part in it. The baby boy being circumcised is only one of the key actors taking part in this very important event. Circumcision definitely has a communal aspect to it without question. Circumcision is an event involving very personal and private issues involving the most private parts of a person's anatomy, but it is done in a way where there is a very specific public recognition and knowledge that the recipient boy has been circumcised and that the public recognizes and witnesses this fact.

To begin, I thought it best to refer to a specific text which serves as a basis for not only what takes place in a physical sense during the ritual and who is involved, but also, most importantly, what is said during the ritual and what the participants are committing to and internalizing in the ritual and to see the goals involved by this ceremony. In my view, in studying this practice, this is really one of the most instructive aspects of the entire ritual.

In this regard, I am going to refer to a main text[19] which is based on several traditions. What is key to understand though is that the elements of this written formulation have key elements which are themselves very ancient as the evidence will show. Note that the Hebrew text is accompanied with an English translation.

---

[19] Taken from here https://www.ritualwell.org/ritual/adapted-traditional-bris-milah-ceremony

"The bris ceremony begins with the *kvatterins*[20] bringing the newborn into the room. When the kvatterins pass the baby to the *sandek rishon*[21],

All present say: בָּרוּךְ הַבָּא!·*(Baruch Ha'ba!)* - Welcome!

The following is said by the parents/*mohel*[22], then repeated by all:

Hear, O Israel, the Lord is our God, the Lord is one.[23]	שְׁמַע יִשְׂרָאֵל ה' אֱלֹהֵינוּ ה' אֶחָד) *(Shemah yisra'el Adonay Eloheynu Adonay eh'khad.)*

Parents/mohel say:

Happy is the one drawn near to dwell in your courts; May we be satisfied by the goodness of your ways.[24]	אַשְׁרֵי תִבְחַר וּתְקָרֵב יִשְׁכֹּן חֲצֵרֶיךָ, נִשְׂבְּעָה בְּטוּב בֵּיתֶךָ קְדֹשׁ ○ הֵיכָלֶךָ
"And God appeared to Abram and said to him: I am God Almighty-walk before me and be perfect. I will set my covenant between me and you and multiply you greatly...[25]	וַיֵּרָא ה' אֶל אַבְרָם וַיֹּאמֶר אֵלָיו נִי אֵל שַׁדַּי הִתְהַלֵּךְ לְפָנַי וֶהְיֵה תָמִים וְאֶתְּנָה בְרִיתִי בֵּינִי וּבֵינֶךָ וְאַרְבֶּה אוֹתְךָ בִּמְאֹד מְאֹד.

---

[20] Yiddish - The woman honored with taking the baby boy from his mother and bringing him to the circumcision room, where she hands him to the kvatter (usually her husband). https://www.chabad.org/search/keyword_cdo/kid/14665/jewish/Kvatterin.htm

[21] "The sandek is the person who holds the baby on his lap during the actual bris milah procedure and is considered the highest honor that can be accorded to somebody at a bris." - https://www.yutorah.org/lectures/lecture.cfm/765164/rabbi-aryeh-lebowitz-sandek-at-a-bris-milah/

[22] The ritual circumciser. The one performing the rite of circumcision.

[23] Deuteronomy 6:4

[24] Psalm 65:4

[25] Genesis 17:1-2

| And I will establish my covenant between me and you. And your offspring after you, an everlasting covenant: to be a God to you and your offspring after you."[26] | וַהֲקִמֹתִי אֶת בְּרִיתִי בֵּינִי וּבֵינֶךָ וּבֵין זַרְעֲךָ אַחֲרֶיךָ לְדֹרֹתָם לִבְרִית עוֹלָם לִהְיוֹת לְךָ לֵאלֹהִים, וּלְזַרְעֲךָ אַחֲרֶיךָ . |

The sandek rishon sits with the baby beside the empty Chair of _Elijah_.

Parents/mohel say:

This is the chair of Elijah the prophet.	זֶה הַכִּסֵּא שֶׁל אֵלִיָּהוּ הַנָּבִיא, זָכוּר לַטּוֹב
I long for your salvation, God, and	לִישׁוּעָתְךָ קִוִּיתִי ה',
I have done what is commanded.	שִׁבַּרְתִּי לִישׁוּעָתְךָ ה' וּמִצְוֹתֶיךָ עָשִׂיתִי
Elijah, messenger of the covenant,	אֵלִיָּהוּ מַלְאַךְ הַבְּרִית הִנֵּה שֶׁלְּךָ לְפָנֶיךָ
stand by my side and assist me.	עֲמוֹד עַל יְמִינִי וְסָמְכֵנִי
I rejoice in your words as in treasure.	שָׂשׂ אָנֹכִי עַל אִמְרָתֶךָ כְּמוֹצֵא שָׁלָל רָב.
May we abound in peace and stumble not.	שָׁלוֹם רָב לְאֹהֲבֵי תוֹרָתֶךָ וְאֵין לָמוֹ מִכְשׁוֹל
Happy is the one drawn near to dwell in your courts; May we be satisfied by the goodness of your ways.[27]	אַשְׁרֵי תִּבְחַר וּתְקָרֵב יִשְׁכֹּן חֲצֵרֶיךָ, נִשְׂבְּעָה בְּטוּב בֵּיתֶךָ קְדֹשׁ הֵיכָלֶךָ

Parents/mohel recite:

| Here I am, ready to perform the commandment | הִנְנִי מוּכָן וּמְזֻמָּן לְקַיֵּם מִצְוַת עֲשֵׂה |

---

[26] Genesis 17:7
[27] Psalm 65:4

that the Creator has commanded us, to circumcise.	שֶׁצִּוָּנוּ הַבּוֹרֵא יִתְבָּרַךְ לָמוֹל

The mohel asks the parents for permission to act on their behalf. He then recites the blessing on the circumcision:

Blessed are you, Lord, our God,	בָּרוּךְ אַתָּה ה' אֱלֹהֵינוּ מֶלֶךְ הָעוֹלָם
who has commanded us regarding circumcision.	אֲשֶׁר קִדְּשָׁנוּ בְּמִצְוֹתָיו וְצִוָּנוּ עַל הַמִּילָה

The mohel performs the circumcision (*milah*).

When he finishes the *milah*, the **parents say:**

Blessed are you, Lord, our God,	בָּרוּךְ אַתָּה ה' אֱלֹהֵינוּ מֶלֶךְ הָעוֹלָם
who has commanded us	אֲשֶׁר קִדְּשָׁנוּ בְּמִצְוֹתָיו וְצִוָּנוּ
to bring him into the covenant of Abraham our father.	לְהַכְנִיסוֹ בִּבְרִיתוֹ שֶׁל אַבְרָהָם אָבִינוּ

All present respond:

Amen. Just as he has entered into the covenant, so may he enter Torah, the marriage canopy, and good deeds!	אָמֵן. כְּשֵׁם שֶׁנִּכְנַס לַבְּרִית, כֵּן יִכָּנֵס לַתּוֹרָה! וּלְחוּפָּה וּלְמַעֲשִׂים טוֹבִים

When the mohel finishes the circumcision, the *sandek rishon* passes the baby to the *sandek sheni* (*second most honored person).

The **parents** take a glass of wine in their right hand and **recite the following blessings:**

Blessed are you, Lord, our God,	בָּרוּךְ אַתָּה ה׳ אֱלֹהֵינוּ מֶלֶךְ הָעוֹלָם
who creates the fruit of the vine.	בּוֹרֵא פְּרִי הַגָּפֶן
Blessed are you, Lord, our God, who	בָּרוּךְ אַתָּה ה׳ אֱלֹהֵינוּ מֶלֶךְ הָעוֹלָם
has sanctified this beloved boy from the womb,	אֲשֶׁר קִדַּשׁ יָדִיד מִבֶּטֶן,
inscribed the law in his flesh,	וְצֶאֱצָאָיו חָתַם וְחוֹק בִּשְׁאֵרוֹ שָׂם
and sealed his offspring in the holy covenant.	בָּאוֹת בְּרִית קֹדֶשׁ
The living God, our Rock, has ordained that	עַל כֵּן בִּשְׂכַר זֹאת אֵל חַי חֶלְקֵנוּ צוּרֵנוּ
the beloved of our flesh be redeemed on account	צִוָּה לְהַצִּיל יְדִידוּת שְׁאֵרֵנוּ מִשַּׁחַת
of the covenant that he has placed in our flesh.	לְמַעַן בְּרִיתוֹ אֲשֶׁר שָׂם בִּבְשָׂרֵנוּ
Blessed are you, God, who makes the covenant.	בָּרוּךְ אַתָּה ה׳ כּוֹרֵת הַבְּרִית

The baby is named:

Our God and the God of our forefathers,	אֱלֹהֵינוּ וֵאלֹהֵי אֲבוֹתֵינוּ,
sustain this child for his father and mother and may he be called in Israel [...].	קַיֵּם אֶת הַיֶּלֶד הַזֶּה לְאָבִיו וּלְאִמּוֹ וְיִקָּרֵא שְׁמוֹ בְּיִשְׂרָאֵל פלוני בן פלוני ופלונית.
May his parents rejoice in him, as it's written:	יִשְׂמַח הָאָב בְּיוֹצֵא חֲלָצָיו,
"May your parents rejoice and she who bore you exult."	וְתָגֵל אִמּוֹ בִּפְרִי בִטְנָהּ
And it's said: Here is God's apportionment - children. And it's said:	כַּכָּתוּב: יִשְׂמַח אָבִיךָ וְאִמֶּךָ וְתָגֵל יוֹלַדְתֶּךָ וְנֶאֱמַר: הִנֵּה נַחֲלַת ה׳ בָּנִים, שָׂכָר פְּרִי הַבָּטֶן.

24

"Trust God. Let Him save and delight in it.	
You delivered me from the womb; you made me trust.	וְנֶאֱמַר: גֹּל אֶל ה' יְפַלְּטֵהוּ יַצִּילֵהוּ כִּי חָפֵץ בּוֹ
from upon my mother's breasts. I have been cast upon.	כִּי אַתָּה גֹחִי מִבָּטֶן, מַבְטִיחִי עַל שְׁדֵי אִמִּי
you from birth; from the womb you are my God.".	עָלֶיךָ הָשְׁלַכְתִּי מֵרָחֶם; מִבֶּטֶן אִמִּי אֵלִי אָתָּה
And it's said: "He forever remembered the covenant, which	וְנֶאֱמַר: זָכַר לְעוֹלָם בְּרִיתוֹ
which He made to Abraham, and swore to Isaac, and established for Jacob as a law and to Israel as an eternal covenant."	דָּבָר צִוָּה לְאֶלֶף דּוֹר אֲשֶׁר כָּרַת אֶת אַבְרָהָם, וּשְׁבוּעָתוֹ לְיִצְחָק , וַיַּעֲמִידֶהָ לְיַעֲקֹב לְחוֹק, לְיִשְׂרָאֵל בְּרִית עוֹלָם
And it's said: "And Abraham circumcised Isaac his son at the age of eight days as God commanded him."	וְנֶאֱמַר: וַיָּמָל אַבְרָהָם אֶת יִצְחָק בְּנוֹ בֶּן שְׁמֹנַת יָמִים כַּאֲשֶׁר צִוָּה אֹתוֹ אֱלֹהִים
And it's said: "According to the kindness I have done	וְנֶאֱמַר: כַּחֶסֶד אֲשֶׁר עָשִׂיתִי עִמְּךָ
for you, so shall you do for me."	תַּעֲשֶׂה עִמָּדִי

The following is **said by the parents/mohel, then repeated by all, twice:**

Give thanks to God for He is good; His kindness is forever.	הוֹדוּ לַה' כִּי טוֹב, כִּי לְעוֹלָם חַסְדּוֹ

The parents continue:

May this little one [...] become great.	(פְּלוֹנִי) זֶה הַקָּטָן, גָּדוֹל יִהְיֶה
Just as he has entered the covenant, so may he enter Torah, the marriage canopy, and good deeds.	כְּשֵׁם שֶׁנִּכְנַס לַבְּרִית, כֵּן יִכָּנֵס לְתוֹרָה וּלְחוּפָּה וּלְמַעֲשִׂים טוֹבִים.
May it be so, amen.	וְכֵן יְהִי רָצוֹן, וְנֹאמַר אָמֵן

The **parents** now drink the wine. They then **recite the following prayer:**

Lord of the world, may it be your will that this	רִבּוֹנוֹ שֶׁל עוֹלָם, יְהִי רָצוֹן מִלְּפָנֶיךָ
be considered and accepted as though	שֶׁיְּהֵא זֶה חָשׁוּב וּמְקֻבָּל לְפָנֶיךָ
he was brought before the throne of your glory.	כְּאִלּוּ הִקְרַבְתִּיהוּ לִפְנֵי כִסֵּא כְבוֹדֶךָ
And may you in your abundant mercy send a pure soul to	וְאַתָּה, בְּרַחֲמֶיךָ הָרַבִּים, שְׁלַח עַל יְדֵי
	מַלְאָכֶיךָ הַקְּדוֹשִׁים נְשָׁמָה קְדוֹשָׁה וּטְהוֹרָה
[...] who was circumcised just now,	לְ(פְּלוֹנִי), הַנִּמּוֹל עַתָּה לְשִׁמְךָ הַגָּדוֹל,
and may his heart be open	וְשֶׁיִּהְיֶה לִבּוֹ פָּתוּחַ כְּפִתְחוֹ שֶׁל אוּלָם
to your holy Torah:	בְּתוֹרָתְךָ הַקְּדוֹשָׁה
to study and teach, to observe and perform.	לִלְמוֹד וּלְלַמֵּד, לִשְׁמוֹר וְלַעֲשׂוֹת
And give him long days and years,	וְתֶן לוֹ אֲרִיכוּת יָמִים וְשָׁנִים,
a life of piety and richness and honor,	חַיִּים שֶׁל יִרְאַת חֵטְא, חַיִּים שֶׁל עוֹשֶׁר וְכָבוֹד,
and may the depths of his heart be filled with good.	וְשֶׁתְּמַלֵּא מִשְׁאֲלוֹת לִבּוֹ לְטוֹבָה
Amen, and may it be so.	אָמֵן, וְכֵן יְהִי רָצוֹן.

The mother recites the following *tekhine (Yiddish meaning 'devotion')*:

Lord of the world, when the Temple stood in Jerusalem a woman who had just risen from childbirth was obligated to bring a sacrifice.	רבונו של עולם, ווען דאס בית המקדש איז געשטאנען אין ירושלים האט איין יולדת בעדארפט אויפשטיינדיג פון קינדבעט ברענגען א קרבן.
Now that the Temple is no more, one fulfills this obligation with prayer in a lesser temple.	איצט, בעבור עוונותינו הרבים, אז דאס בית המקדש איז ניטא, איז מען יוצא מיט די תפילה אין מקדש מעט.
So I come to shul to thank you, dear God,	גיי איך אין שול דיר, ליבער גאט,
and to praise you for all the lovingkindness	דאנקען און לויבן פאר אלץ וואס
that you have bestowed upon me to this day.	דו האסט מיט מיר ביז היינט געטאן חסד
And I also ask you not to cease performing	און איך בעט דיר דאס וויטער
your lovingkindness for me:	זאלסטו אויך דיין חסד ניט אפ טאן פון מיר:
May [...] be a beautiful sapling	פלוני זאל זיין א שיינע פלאנצונג אין
in the Jewish vineyard, for the glory of Israel.	דעם יידישן וויינגארטן, לתפארת ישראל.
May he come into the world to help	ער זאל קומען אויף דער וועלט
bring salvation and comfort to all Israel.	צוא ישועות ונחמות אויף כלל ישראל.
In his time may the Jews merit	אין זיין צייט זאלין יידן
a true redemption, amen.	זוכה זיין א וואַרע גאולה, אמן.

27

All sing:

May the angel who has delivered me from all harm bless the young, and may they carry on my name and the name of our forefathers Abraham and Isaac, and may they multiply throughout the earth.	הַמַּלְאָךְ הַגּוֹאֵל אוֹתִי, הַמַּלְאָךְ הַגּוֹאֵל אוֹתִי יְבָרֵךְ אֶת הַנְּעָרִים, וְיִקָּרֵא בָהֶם שְׁמִי מִכָּל רָע וְשֵׁם אֲבֹתַי, וְשֵׁם אֲבֹתַי, אַבְרָהָם וְיִצְחָק, וְיִדְגּוּ לָרֹב, וְיִדְגּוּ לָרֹב, בְּקֶרֶב הָאָרֶץ.

Mother recites the following blessing of thanks:

Blessed are you, Lord, our God, bestower of kindness on those in need, for bestowing every kindness upon me.	בָּרוּךְ אַתָּה ה' אֱלֹהֵינוּ מֶלֶךְ הָעוֹלָם הַגּוֹמֵל לְחַיָּבִים טוֹבוֹת שֶׁגְּמָלַנִי כָּל טוֹב

All respond:

May the one who has bestowed upon you every kindness bestow upon you every kindness forever.	מִי שֶׁגְּמָלֵךְ כָּל טוֹב, הוּא יִגְמָלֵךְ כָּל טוֹב, סֶלָה

Mohel recites the following:

He who blessed our forefathers Abraham, Isaac and Jacob, Moses, Aaron, David and Solomon, may He bless the tender boy [...] on account of his being entered into the covenant.	מִי שֶׁבֵּרַךְ אֲבוֹתֵינוּ אַבְרָהָם יִצְחָק וְיַעֲקֹב, מֹשֶׁה וְאַהֲרֹן דָּוִד וּשְׁלֹמֹה, הוּא יְבָרֵךְ אֶת הַיֶּלֶד רַךְ הַנִּימוֹל פְּלוֹנִי בֶּן פְּלוֹנִי וּפְלוֹנִית בַּעֲבוּר שֶׁנִּכְנַס לַבְּרִית
May God send him a full and speedy recovery.	בִּשְׂכַר זֶה הַקָּדוֹשׁ בָּרוּךְ הוּא יִשְׁלַח לוֹ

| And may He raise him towards Torah, the marriage canopy, and good deeds, and let us say, amen. | מְהֵרָה רְפוּאָה שְׁלֵמָה בְּכָל רַמַ''ח אֵבָרָיו וּשְׁסַ''ה גִידָיו וִיגַדְלוּהוּ לְתוֹרָה, וּלְחֻפָּה, וּלְמַעֲשִׂים טוֹבִים, וְנֹאמַר, אָמֵן. |

Priestly blessing is recited:

May God bless and protect you.	יְבָרֶכְךָ ה' וְיִשְׁמְרֶךָ,
May God shine his face upon you and be gracious to you.	יָאֵר ה' פָּנָיו אֵלֶיךָ וִיחֻנֶּךָ,
May God turn to you and grant you peace.	יִשָּׂא ה' פָּנָיו אֵלֶיךָ וְיָשֵׂם לְךָ שָׁלוֹם.

The baby is passed to the kvatterins and exits the room.

All are welcome to join for a festive meal." (End of the ceremony)

Comments on the ceremony as referenced in this text:

To best understand circumcision, it is helpful to study with some care the ceremony and what is said in the ceremony so that we can better understand what is taking place, why it is happening and what is it designed to achieve.

The ceremony begins with the holiest of all texts in the Torah, which is Deuteronomy 6:4:

"Hear, O Israel, the Lord is our God, the Lord is one." (ESV)

Next, we have a quotation from Psalm 65:4 saying:

"Happy is the one drawn near to dwell in your courts; May we be satisfied by the goodness of your ways."

This text helps to show the rationale and necessity for circumcision. Circumcision became a requirement for all Jewish males to be able to come into God's presence in the Temple when it was in existence. To be able to approach God and to "draw near to dwell in your courts", this was only possible for circumcised men.

Next, we have two of the key texts from Genesis 17 concerning circumcision:

"And God appeared to Abram and said to him: I am God Almighty-walk before me and be perfect. I will set my covenant between me and you and multiply you greatly..." (Genesis 17:1,2)

"And I will establish my covenant between me and you. And your offspring after you, an everlasting covenant: to be a God to you and your offspring after you." (Genesis 17:7)

We note in these texts that there is a focus on the necessity of this ceremony to "walk before me" and the need to "be perfect." In addition, we note the emphasis on the covenantal nature of the relationship and how those who are a part of this covenant will see their numbers in the world to "multiply you greatly." Notice again the mention of "your offspring" and "your offspring after you." The fundamental nature of the relationship is one of great holiness and solemnity because the LORD says that He will "be a God to you." No more important relationship can be imagined between God and mankind and this is being emphasized in the circumcision ceremony.

Next, we see reference to Elijah the prophet and some further benediction concerning the fact that the parents are following God's instructions and His commandment by doing the circumcision.

Then the circumcision takes place and a blessing is recited towards the LORD concerning His commandment of circumcision.

Then, the assembled people say: "Amen" and mention that the child who has entered the covenant of circumcision, it is now the hope that he will enter "Torah, the marriage canopy and good deeds."

This is an important commentary because it helps to show the rationale for circumcision. It is the desire of the parents and the community that this child embrace and follow Torah. In doing that, he would desire to marry and complete the first commandment found in the Bible (to have children – Genesis 1:28) after which hopefully this child would then pursue good deeds in life.

Then, the parents recite another blessing accompanied by a glass of wine in the right hand. This blessing acknowledges God as the creator of the fruit of the vine and who has sanctified the child from the womb and inscribed in his flesh the law (Torah) and sealed the child in the holy covenant.

The baby is then named and further blessings and thanksgivings are pronounced.

Then God is thanked twice for His goodness and kindness. Then, the parents once again recite the formulation that the boy enter Torah, the marriage canopy and good deeds.

A final blessing is recited by the parents who drink the wine. This focuses on asking God to bless the child, to send to him a pure soul that he be open to study, teach and observe the Torah and that he have a long and blessed and fruitful life.

Then, the child's mother recites a thanksgiving blessing after which all ask God to bless the child by continuing the family name linking back to the patriarch Abraham and that the people of God would multiply throughout the earth.

Then the child's mother again thanks God for the kindness showed to her to be the mother of the child after which those in attendance affirm this thanksgiving prayer.

Then, the mohel, who performed the circumcision asks God's blessing on the boy in the name of the Jewish people's forefathers wishing the child a speedy recovery and finally mentions again towards the Torah, the marriage canopy and good deeds.

In conclusion, we are going to see that this ceremony focuses on bringing the child into the covenant of Abraham with the focus on living a life focused on and motivated by the Torah with the importance focused on getting married obviously to a holy and righteous woman and following through and living a holy life of good deeds that gives glory to God and to His Holy Torah.

The idea of sanctification is present in the circumcision and the focus on this being an event which starts the child off in a life based on holy living, purity and a movement towards having his own righteous family in the future. This provides us a good basis to move forward in our investigation of circumcision and its meaning.

4.   Circumcision: Understanding its link to sexual ethics

To begin a discussion about the teaching of circumcision, it is reasonable to establish a foundation concerning how one looks in particular at the book of Genesis, where this teaching is first found. Depending on one's orientation towards the material in Genesis, this could affect how one looked at the teaching of circumcision.

In this book, we are going to take the view that the book of Genesis is inspired Scripture as much as any other book found in the Hebrew Bible or the Christian New Testament. In this regard, Dr. Bullinger made the following remark:

"Genesis is the seed-plot of the whole Bible. It is essential to the true understanding of its every part. It is the foundation of which Divine Revelation rests; and on which it is built up. It is not only the foundation of all Truth, but it enters into, and forms part of all subsequent inspiration.

Genesis is quoted or referred to sixty times in the New Testament; and Divine authority is set like a seal on its historical facts. See Matt.19:4-6; 24:37-39; Mark 7:4, 10; 10:3-8; Luke 11:43-51; 17:28, 29, 32; John 1:51; 7:21-23; 8:44-56.

It and the Book of the Law, of which it forms part, are ascribed to Moses. See Deut. 31:9,10, 24-26; Josh. 1:7; 8:32,35; 23:6; I Kings 2:3; II Kings 14:6; 23:25; II Chron. 23:18; 30:16; 34:14; Ezra 3:2; 7:6; Neh. 8:1; Dan. 9:11,13; Mal. 4:4; Mark 12:26; Luke 2:22; John 7:23; Acts 13:39; 15:5; 28:23; I Cor. 9:9; Hebrews 10:28."[28]

The point of view expressed by Dr. Bullinger is that exactly taken in this book. Having said this, however, in Genesis we encounter the teaching of circumcision

---

[28] Bullinger, E.W. The Companion Bible. Lamp Press: London, Appendix 3, Pg.

and make no mistake about it, circumcision is a difficult Bible teaching to understand for anyone.

It is really hard to fathom why the LORD would ever suggest that such a procedure be undertaken on anyone, especially on boy babies only eight days old. It is very difficult to fathom God's mind on this issue. Why would He ever suggest this ritual?

To me, on the surface, the whole idea seems to be somewhat strange and extreme. On the surface, when you read the accounts in the Bible where this practice is mentioned, on the surface, it all just seems a bit strange and very difficult to understand it in a logical and practical way. But here is where we really need to look at the whole counsel of God to find out what this subject really means. It does have a meaning that we can ascertain if we are willing to study it through carefully.

**We must remove our feelings on circumcision
from our desire to understand it**

When St. Paul went to Athens to speak to the philosophers, he did so from their point of view. He did not speak to them from his point of view. He addressed them talking about "the Unknown God" (Acts 17:23) Today, many people look at the subject of circumcision and find it to be a teaching of an unknown God. They find it so hard to understand, appreciate and respect. It appears on the surface to be brutal, barbaric, extreme and mysterious.

This idea is not new and we find individuals even in the Bible expressing their astonishment and revulsion at the teaching of circumcision. Recall the reaction of the wife of Moses, Zipporah, as mentioned in Exodus 4:25 saying:

"Then Zipporah took a flint and cut off her son's foreskin and threw it at Moses' feet, and she said, "You are indeed a bridegroom of blood to me." (NASB)

There is clearly a tension that goes against our intuition with this teaching of circumcision. It can make us feel uncomfortable and appears barbaric according to our modern sensibilities. Yes, this is often how this teaching makes people (especially Christians) feel who have not studied the circumcision issue carefully.

To develop a correct, mature and biblically accurate understanding of circumcision, we must keep in mind certain ideas. If we do this, we are going to be on the right path towards an accurate understanding of this or any teaching of the Bible.

The first idea we have to remember is that God is love. (I John 4:8) Because God does not change, we must believe that God loved the world (and everything in the world, of course, especially humanity) in the past, loves the world now and will love the world in the future. The key passage in this regard is John 3:16,17. We need to understand that the LORD gave humanity circumcision because He loves us and because He only wishes good for His children. God is Love. Everything He does is because of love including circumcision.

Next, we must believe that God would not give a teaching to mankind as a commandment, as circumcision is, which is not for humankinds' benefit. Matthew 7:8-11 shows that God gives good things to humanity. This is certainly not easy for us when it comes to the issue of circumcision, but here we must, I believe, put aside our modern gut level reactions to the teaching no matter how it makes us feel on the surface and admit that this is something which is good from God and it represents a good gift to humanity for their benefit. This becomes possible when we take ourselves back into history and look at the whole situation of what was taking place up until the time circumcision was finally revealed by God to Abraham. When we look at circumcision from the point of view of that situation taking place at that time, we can have a much better understanding of why God would introduce a practice like circumcision in the first place. Mankind needed something urgently at that time to reorient the society towards holiness and right living. These virtues were in very short supply at that time and the whole society was in a situation which God found 100% intolerable and unacceptable for humanity's proper well-being and growth in a way that followed God's design for holy living and for the proper development of society.

Finally, we must understand that our reaction to the teachings that we find in the Bible does not represent a deficiency on the part of the LORD. No! The deficiency, if one exists, only comes about due to the lack of understanding of humanity! Psalm 19 teaches us that the Bible, the Law of the Lord, is perfect. It gives wisdom, understanding, its testimonies are right. This is the attitude we need to have about the Holy Scriptures knowing that God's ways and man's ways are not always congruent, but in every case, God ways are those to be preferred. We must trust the LORD that He knows what He is doing. (Proverbs 3:5-7)

If we agree with these approaches, we are going to find ourselves much more at ease when it comes to Biblical teachings, like circumcision, that may make our modern sensibilities uncomfortable. This is where we need to trust the LORD, and not lean on our own understanding. He has our best interests at heart as He, the exponent of supreme Love, demonstrates this in His actions time and again as revealed in His Holy Scriptures.

Moving Towards Redemption Through the Biblical Text

How we look at a Bible text makes all the difference in the world. Our attitude towards a text needs to be mature. We need to put away childish things when it comes to the Bible. (I Corinthians 13:11) In this research study, we wish to utilize a methodology to help us appreciate and better understand circumcision. This methodology is known as Redemptive Movement Hermeneutic (RMH). In this regard, we will utilize the RMH model of Prof. William Webb in his excellent book "Bloody, Brutal and Barbaric?" (IVP Academic) to help us better understand the teaching of circumcision. Let us look now at a descriptive graphic that Prof. Webb has graciously permitted me to reference here:

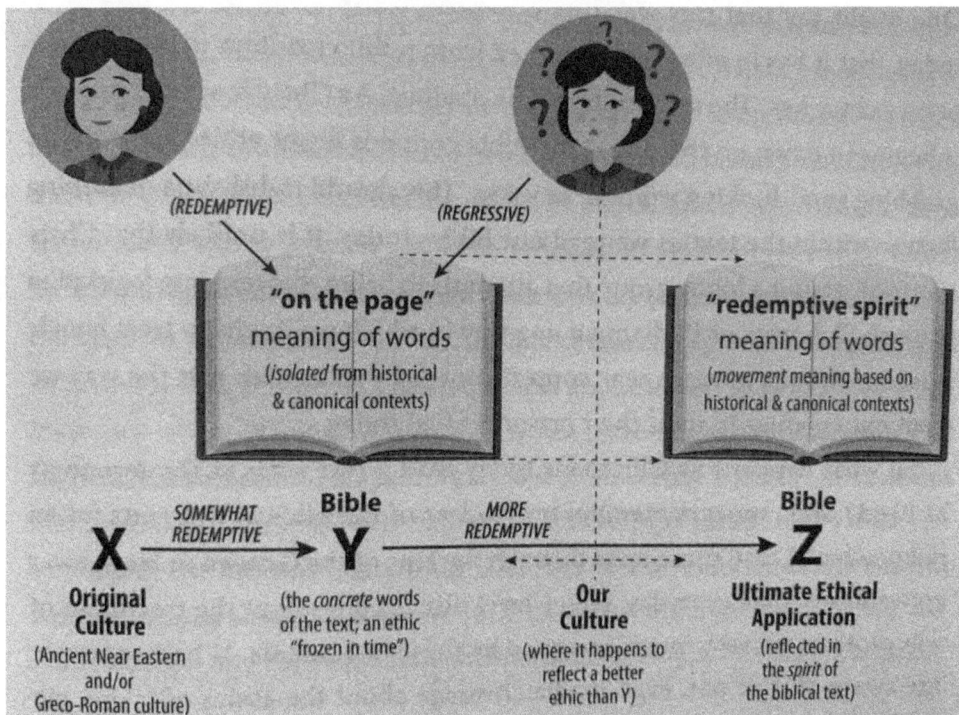

(REDEMPTIVE)   *(REGRESSIVE)*

"on the page" meaning of words (*isolated* from historical & canonical contexts)

"redemptive spirit" meaning of words (*movement* meaning based on historical & canonical contexts)

SOMEWHAT REDEMPTIVE   **Bible**   MORE REDEMPTIVE   **Bible**

X ⟶ **Y** ⟶ **Z**

Original Culture (Ancient Near Eastern and/or Greco-Roman culture)

(the *concrete* words of the text; an ethic "frozen in time")

Our Culture (where it happens to reflect a better ethic than Y)

Ultimate Ethical Application (reflected in the *spirit* of the biblical text)

When we look at this graphic, the first picture to look at is of the woman mid center who is looking at a Bible text and questioning it in a very troubling way. Her view of the text is that it is regressive. It is painful to read. When she reads this text on the page comparing it to her own personal understanding, it is regressive and appears to be brutal and barbaric. This is how many Christians today look at the teaching of circumcision. It looks to be brutal and barbaric from their point of view. And they are right! From their point of view, it is brutal and barbaric, but she needs to ask herself this question: "Will this approach lead me to the truth to understand an ancient teaching in the Bible?"

Now, look at the woman on the left who is looking at the exact same text. Why is she happy? This is because she sees what is taking place around her at that time and when she looks at this text, she is happy. She is happy because she sees where God is leading us. She sees a God who is leading us to redemption slowly through a progressive revelation slowly revealing more and more of Himself and because of this she is not sad. She understands the teaching that was given by God at the time it was given and in the cultural background where it was given and looks at it on the basis of what was taking place at that time. She does not bring in her modern point of view looking back like the other woman. When she does this, she forms a point of view based on God's introduction of a new teaching. This is why she understands better and rightly appreciates how God is engaging with humanity in history. She sees the love of God in action and feels happy. What we are going to find is that circumcision was introduced at a time where mankind was definitely moving in the wrong direction and a serious teaching to reorient mankind back towards God's design for holiness was required.

The introduction of the teaching of Circumcision:
Pay attention to the context

It is not often mentioned in studying the subject of circumcision that it is the second of the suggested body of 613 commandments obligatory on the religious Jewish person (Hebrew: *mitzvot*) found in the Torah. There are, in fact, some 16 chapters between the first and the second commandments. The first commandment of the 613 commandments is found in Genesis 1:28:

"Be fruitful and multiply; and fill the earth, and subdue it."

Now, this process involves the normal function of human reproduction. Sexual relationships between males and females are part of fulfilling this commandment. But what kind of sexual relationships? One does not have to read very far in the book of Genesis to learn what types of sexual relationships God approves of and those which are the best for the society which God wishes humanity to have and are in conformity to God's design for a holy society. (Gen. 2:24)

What we are going to find is, in fact, there is a much greater link to a progressive revelation[29] of sexual ethics that God has placed on human beings to be in conformity to His divine will that starts here in Genesis 1:28, is further defined in Genesis 2:24 and then comes up again and starts to be more defined in Genesis 17 with the teaching of circumcision.[30] What we have to realize is that God is progressively revealing Himself to mankind in a step-by-step fashion and this also concerns the issue of sexual ethics and the moral behavior of mankind.

What we are going to find is that God, while He wants mankind to fulfill Genesis 1:28, He wishes that commandment to be adhered to using principles which He has revealed to mankind in His Holy Word. The teaching of circumcision was a foundational one that was understood by early Jews to be linked very much to the human male's sexual ethical behavior. It is no accident

---

[29] "Let us first understand the intent of the phrase. By "progressive" we do not mean "modern" or "liberal." We are using it in the sense of something being passed successively from one point of a series to the next. Or, even more definitely, "to progress step-by-step towards improvement until a desired higher plane of development is reached." (quoting E. L. Martin, Progressive Revelation, FBR: Pasadena: CA, 1974)

[30] It is important to note also that there is another direct link between this verse and the commandment to procreate and that of circumcision. This is because both of these commandments were only required for men, not for women. See Rabbi Abraham Chill, The Mitzvot: The Commandments and their Rationale: Keter Books: Jerusalem, 1974, pg. 3.

that the male generative organ was selected by the LORD to be the location for this ritual to be administered.

What we find the LORD teaching us is the importance of holy behavior of men and their role in producing a holy society. The entire society has a role in this and this is why circumcision was introduced into the society because it was a sign that the parents of the boy in question were going to raise him up in conformity with proper sexual ethics and later linked to all the teachings of Moses' Law (including right and legal sexual practices) and in doing so, he would be a suitable mate to his wife for the future perpetuation of a holy society. Keeping this essential covenant ensured all the members of the society were seeking to pursue holiness and a desire to perpetuate a holy and godly society. Rabbinical scholars agree with this suggestion. Note Rabbi Abarbanel's comments about circumcision in general:

"Furthermore, if this organ, (speaking of the male generative organ) which is the source of physical pleasure, is sanctified through circumcision, then the children whom he will eventually beget will be conceived in holiness." (*ibid.*, Chill, p. 6)

Circumcision, therefore, is presented as a requirement to the Patriarch Abraham. We are all familiar with the story of how it comes into being. This story is found in Genesis 17. However, there are two very important stories that are a part of the narrative of the life of Abraham which are linked to the introduction of circumcision.

In this regard, it is important to understand something about humanity which the Bible reveals in the earlier period before Abraham received the covenant of circumcision. Here we have to return even back to a time before the

40

cataclysmic destruction of Noah (commonly known as the Flood), where we see a serious degradation in the behavior of humanity, where the LORD says:

"The LORD saw that the wickedness of man was great in the earth, and that every intention of the thoughts of his heart was only evil continually. And the LORD regretted that he had made man on the earth, and it grieved him to his heart." (Genesis 6:5-6 ESV)

Certainly, the LORD does point out his favor concerning Noah (whose name means "comfort" or "rest" in Hebrew), but even after the Flood, we find one of Noah's first recorded acts to involve actions which were recognized even in that time as outside of the boundaries of godly living. (Genesis 9:21)

The teaching of Circumcision is linked to what happened to Noah

The circumstances of what happened to Noah are quite uncomfortable to discuss. This story is a part of the Holy Scripture, so there is no reason not to discuss it maturely and academically. Let us review what the Scriptures mention:

"Then Noah began farming and planted a vineyard. He drank of the wine and became drunk, and uncovered himself inside his tent. Ham, the father of Canaan, saw the nakedness of his father, and told his two brothers outside. But Shem and Japheth took a garment and laid it upon both their shoulders and walked backward and covered the nakedness of their father; and their faces were turned away, so that they did not see their father's nakedness. When Noah awoke from his wine, he knew what his youngest son had done to him. So he said, 'Cursed be Canaan; A servant of servants He shall be to his brothers'." (Gen. 9:20-25 NASB)

41

When we review what ancient rabbinical commentators[31] talk about three main ideas come to mind. These are:

1. That Noah was emasculated by the son of Ham, Canaan
2. That Noah was defiled (indulged his perverted lust) by Ham's son, Canaan
3. That both of these things happened

Whatever happened exactly, we cannot be 100% certain, but when we look at this story in the context of the first 18 chapters of Genesis, it definitely follows in the theme of Genesis 6:5-6, which was quoted earlier. It could very well highlight inappropriate sexual relations between two males. This seems to be the case based not only on Genesis 9 but also on the whole context of the first 18 chapters of Genesis leading up to the introduction of Abraham. But the moral failure did not end with Noah.

It is here though important to point out that the LORD then introduces the subject of the tower of Babel (which in Hebrew means "confusion or mixing"). When we read the narrative of the tower, we need to pay attention to it on a number of levels and one of these involves circumcision. What we find, if we are willing to pay close attention to it, is that herein in this story of the tower of Babel, there is also a message of unethical human behavior initiated by men and this is reflected in the symbolism of the tower. This idea is reiterated by the late Dr. Ernest L. Martin saying:

"THE BIBLE records that in the earliest ages, right after the Flood of Noah, men began to rebel against the teachings of God. They began to build cities, found

---

[31] It is also mentioned that due to the use of the Hebrew word 'tent' אֹהֶל, one Rabbi believed Noah was in his wife's tent based on the use of this word and the phrase "his fathers' nakedness" refers to Noah's wife. See Leviticus 18:8 where a similar formulation is used.

religions, bring in idolatries. Pagan temples were erected -- the Tower of Babel came on the scene. All of these things started within the first two hundred years after the Flood."[32]

Dr. Martin continues:

"In the Bible, however, the first-time people on the earth wanted to make such a tower that looked like it reached to heaven, God got angry with them. He came down and confused their language and sent people into all areas of the world for their rebellion to Him in raising up such a tower." (Genesis 11:1-9).

But what is wrong with a tower? A tower in and of itself is not the problem. It is what the tower meant and signified in a religious sense and this is the reason that the LORD confounded the languages of mankind and scattered the people over the whole face of the earth. And what did the tower signify? Dr. Martin comments on this issue with reference to clear classical historical fact.

"But why should anyone want to raise up towers in the first place in association with places of religious worship? The use of towers stemmed from the practice in early Egypt of erecting obelisks as sacred shrines or monuments near or at their places of worship. But why have such towers with various shapes (but almost all of them displayed as long, erect and normally with a type of point or pyramid on top like our steeples and spires)?

Classical history is clear on this matter. When the Egyptian God Osiris was killed and dismembered (with his body parts scattered around the country), the Goddess Isis (his sister and wife) sent her messengers to gather the body parts together for a proper burial of Osiris. They were successful in discovering all the parts of the body except the penis. They looked all over for it, but it was never

---

[32] www.reformation.org/simon_peter_versus_simon_magus.html - (E. Martin, "Simon Magus")

43

found. So what did Isis do? She erected various kinds of obelisks always erect and upright in a type of penis-form to remind the people to look for Osiris' lost penis. To not let them forget it, she erected numerous obelisks penis-like monuments at the main places of Egyptian worship (Diodorus Siculus, Book I, Chap. Two). As a matter of fact, the Egyptians gave the practice to the Greeks and then it came to the Romans."

Continuing:

"The Romans even transported to Rome some of these Egyptian obelisks for their own worship purposes. Following the example of the Egyptian Goddess Isis, the practice of raising up obelisks in the form of spires and towers continued throughout the pagan world with various types being used and often their designs were subtlety changed to hide the meaning of what the obelisk actually was.

An important point, however, involves the earliest religious example of a tower-type monument that we are aware of? Of course, it is the tower of Babel.

Dr. Martin concludes saying:

"This example is a biblical story being used with sexual overtones in such religious themes.[33]

Notice in the same chapter where this story is mentioned, the end of the chapter brings us to the introduction of Abram on to the scene. (Genesis 11:26)

---

[33] http://askelm.com/doctrine/d980927.htm - Ernest L. Martin, Anatomy of a Church, Part 1.

Abram was told to remove himself from his former place of living at age 75 and move to another country, which today is the land of Israel. Abram was to separate himself and his family from his former country. Note Genesis 12:1-2:

"Now the LORD said to Abram, 'Go from your country and your kindred and your father's house to the land that I will show you. And I will make of you a great nation, and I will bless you and make your name great, so that you will be a blessing.'" (ESV)

Now, this promise is reiterated with Abram being promised a biological child. (Genesis 15:4) What we find during the time period when Abram left Ur of the Chaldees (which was in fact much closer to the ancient region of Shinar, where the tower of Babel had been) at age 75, for a 24-year period various events happened to him which are mentioned in the Bible from Genesis 13-16. During that period, Abram developed a closer relationship with the LORD and he became a stronger believer in God and His works and His ways. By believing, Abram was considered to be a righteous man in the eyes of God. "And he believed the LORD, and he counted it to him as righteousness." (Genesis 15:6 ESV) However, what the Biblical narrative points to is a further level of righteousness which was going to be required of Abraham and his descendants.

Now, after all of this taking place, we find Chapter 17 of Genesis placed into this context. This section of Scripture deals with the subject of circumcision. It comes after the story of the tower of Babel after which Abram was introduced, taken out of his former country and being brought to a new country and developing a closer relationship with the LORD.

Before we can fully understand the story and reasoning behind circumcision and what it really meant in a Biblical sense, we really need also to understand one other important teaching which was also motivating Abraham and the motivation for this teaching had come also from the LORD.

One thing we can see very clearly in the story of Abram, whose name was changed to Abraham (Genesis 17:5), is his constant desire to have children produced from his own body. You see this mentioned several times in the narratives of Abraham's life.[34] Why was this considered so important to him? This is an important question because it goes back to the first commandment that the LORD ever gave to mankind recorded in the book of Genesis, which is:

"And God blessed them. And God said to them, "Be fruitful and multiply and fill the earth and subdue it, and have dominion over the fish of the sea and over the birds of the heavens and over every living thing that moves on the earth." (Genesis 1:28 ESV)

This command to "be fruitful and multiply" was taken very seriously by early Jewish believers in the Bible, so much so that it became the first commandment of 613 identified in the Bible, which became requirements to be within the divine will of God.

However, in addition to the commandment to reproduce, the LORD defined the way in which this was to be done and this is defined in the first few chapters of the Bible itself. It is precisely through the institution of marriage between a man and a woman from which children are produced. Note the text from Genesis, which points this out:

"Therefore a man shall leave his father and his mother and hold fast to his wife, and they shall become one flesh." (Genesis 2:24 ESV)

---

[34] (Gen. 12:2,7; 13:15,16; 15:2-6; Gen. 16 deals with Ishmael's birth only; 17:4-8; 15-21; 18:9-15)

Now that we can see the overall context from Genesis 11-18 and what are the background elements to the narratives in that section of the Scripture, now we are better positioned to come to a more accurate understanding of **why** the LORD required of Abraham to undertake the ritual of circumcision.

As we have mentioned, there is more to the story of the tower of Babel than the text on the surface presents to us. Such is also the case with the teaching of circumcision and to also appreciate the meaning of the text where circumcision is introduced, we have to also note another story found in Genesis 18:16-21 and this story is one which concerns wrong sexual behavior between human beings and in this case, it is sexual behavior between males that the LORD condemns. We also note earlier in Genesis 13:13 a reference to the wrong sexual behavior of the males of Sodom. Note that women are not specifically mentioned in this text and this is important concerning the issue of circumcision. Why? It is because circumcision is specifically a practice directed to and performed on men only.

So how is the cutting off the male foreskin linked to proper human ethical behavior (in particular among men) in the area of sexuality? This is the question now we are going to consider.

Circumcision and human male sexual ethics

The study of ethics is an important matter for humanity. Ethics is broadly defined as follows:

"Ethics, from ἠθος (Greek: *ethos*) ... in English *moral philosophy*, ... Ethics are related to *law* and *duty*, and to *virtue* and *vice*. ... Moral philosophy, or the science of the relations, rights, and duties by which men are under obligations towards God, themselves, and their fellow creatures. ... Ethics then covers the science of

47

all that is moral, whether it relates to law or action, to God or the create, to the individual or the state. It goes wherever the ideas of right and wrong can enter."[35]

Now, in this research study, we are focusing our questioning on the ethical role of circumcision. What was that ethical role? This is because God commanded Abraham to undertake this physical ritual and Abraham hastily undertook to follow the LORD's direction immediately. (Genesis 17:24-27)

On the surface, the textual description of the circumcision commandment and initiation of the circumcision covenant in Genesis 17 does not seem to have a moral component to it. There is no specific mention of this moral meaning in the text, but this is where we need to study the whole matter of circumcision in the Bible to a greater degree. When we do this, the moral meaning of circumcision becomes much clearer. Let's look at a more scholarly examination of this matter to help us really understand it better. Concerning circumcision, note the following elaboration on the Biblical teaching:

"When first appointed by God, circumcision was expressly set forth as a token of the covenant which God had made with Abraham; and the apostle tells us that Abraham received 'the sign of circumcision as a seal of the righteousness of that faith which he had, being yet uncircumcised.' (Romans 4:11); so that to Abraham it was not only a sign or token of God's covenant, but also an obsignation or certificate that he was in a state of acceptance before he was circumcised. As a Mosaic institution, it was also the sign of the covenant which God made with Israel, which is hence called the 'covenant of circumcision' (Acts 7:8). In consequence of this, it became the medium of access to the privileges of the

---

[35] McLintock and Strongs, Cyclopedia of Biblical, Theological and Ecclesiastical Literature: Harper and Brothers, New York, 1883. Vol. III, Pg. 319.

covenant, and entailed on all who received it an obligation to fulfil the duties which the covenant imposed." (Romans 2:25; 3:1; Galatians 5:3).[36]

So, we can see that this covenant or agreement between God and Abraham had duties and promises that both parties had to fulfil. From the side of God and what He agreed to do as a party to the covenant, we can see this in Genesis 17:

"In a word, it was the token which assured to Abraham and his descendants the promise of the Messiah." (*ibid.* pgs. 351-352)

But on the human side, the meaning was twofold:

"As respects to its (circumcision) meaning, that was symbolical, and the things which it symbolized were two: 1. Consecration to God; and 2. Mental and spiritual purification." (*ibid.*)

Let's review some of the relevant Bible texts that show this. Note first Exodus 6:12-13:

"But Moses said to the LORD, "Behold, the people of Israel have not listened to me. How then shall Pharaoh listen to me, for I am of **uncircumcised** lips?" But the LORD spoke to Moses and Aaron and gave them a charge about the people of Israel and about Pharaoh king of Egypt: to bring the people of Israel out of the land of Egypt. (ESV)

---

[36] McLintock and Strongs, Cyclopedia of Biblical, Theological and Ecclesiastical Literature: Harper and Brothers, New York, 1883. Vol. II, Pg. 352.

"When you come into the land and plant any kind of tree for food, then you shall regard its fruit as **forbidden** (in Hebrew this word means "uncircumcised"). Three years it shall be **forbidden** (in Hebrew this word means "uncircumcised") to you; it must not be eaten. And in the fourth year all its fruit shall be holy, an offering of praise to the LORD. But in the fifth year you may eat of its fruit, to increase its yield for you: I am the LORD your God." (Leviticus 19:23-25 ESV)

"**Circumcise** therefore the **foreskin of your heart**, and be no longer stubborn. For the LORD your God is God of gods and Lord of lords, the great, the mighty, and the awesome God, who is not partial and takes no bribe. He executes justice for the fatherless and the widow, and loves the sojourner, giving him food and clothing." (Deuteronomy 10:16-18 ESV)

"And the LORD your God will **circumcise your heart** and the heart of your offspring, so that you will love the LORD your God with all your heart and with all your soul, that you may live." (Deuteronomy 30:6 ESV)

"Awake, awake, put on your strength, O Zion; put on your beautiful garments, O Jerusalem, the holy city; for there shall no more come into you the **uncircumcised** and the unclean." (Isaiah 52:1 ESV)

"**Circumcise** yourselves to the LORD; **remove the foreskin** of your hearts, O men of Judah and inhabitants of Jerusalem; lest my wrath go forth like fire, and burn with none to quench it, because of the evil of your deeds." (Jer. 4:4 ESV)

"To whom shall I speak and give warning, that they may hear? Behold, their ears are **uncircumcised**, they cannot listen; behold, the word of the LORD is to them an object of scorn; they take no pleasure in it." (Jeremiah 6:10 ESV)

"For **circumcision** indeed is of value if you obey the law, but if you break the law, your **circumcision** becomes **uncircumcision**. So, if a man who is **uncircumcised** keeps the precepts of the law, will not his **uncircumcision** be regarded as **circumcision**? Then he who is physically **uncircumcised** but keeps the law will condemn you who have the written code and **circumcision** but break the law. For no one is a Jew who is merely one outwardly, nor is **circumcision** outward and physical. But a Jew is one inwardly, and **circumcision** is a matter of the heart, by the Spirit, not by the letter. His praise is not from man but from God." (Romans 2:25-29 ESV)

"In him also you were **circumcised** with a **circumcision** made without hands, by putting off the body of the flesh, by the **circumcision** of Christ," (Col. 2:11 ESV)

Let's look at some commentary on these verses to better appreciate how to understand circumcision in the proper spiritual sense. What we are going to find is that circumcision has a much deeper meaning linked to consecration, holiness and an offering of the body to God.

"There was thus involved in the concept of *consecration*, and along with this that of reconciliation, in circumcision; and it was thereby, as Ewald rightly remarks, (*Alterth*, p.95) an offering of the body to Jehovah, which, according to the true meaning of all the offerings, as fully develop and raised to their true elevation by the prophets, had to be presented to him as an offering of the soul. Only as this inner offering was perfectly presented could the obligation to be a priestly kingdom and a holy people be fulfilled."[37]

What we have to understand is what circumcision means is linked very much to what the individual male person will do in an ethical sense with his body (in particular what males will do with their generative organs) and in taking on the responsibilities of this covenant relationship with God, the circumcised man entered into a holy relationship with God agreeing to follow God's laws relative to personal conduct in the area of sexual behavior.

To emphasize the importance of this whole matter, we can see the LORD introducing it as a requirement on infant boys. To introduce such a procedure on an infant child of only eight days absolutely must be understood to point to its necessity and its deep meaning as incumbent not only on the one who received the circumcision, but also incumbent on the entire community who had a role in ensuring that the procedure was undertaken on all Jewish children.

Note the following quote from Rabbi Chill:

"It is incumbent on the father to circumcise his son. If the father cannot perform this act himself, he may appoint a *mohel* as his agent to perform the *mitzvah* for him. If for some reason the father fails to have his son circumcised, it becomes incumbent on the *Bet Din* of the community to see that the circumcision is performed. (Chill, pg. 5)

---

[37] McLintock and Strongs, Cyclopedia of Biblical, Theological and Ecclesiastical Literature: Harper and Brothers, New York, 1883. Vol. II, Pg. 352.

So important, holy and sacrosanct was this ritual that it was to be performed even on the Day of Atonement, which was the holiest day in the Hebrew calendar. (*ibid*. Chill, pg. 5) This just shows how important this matter was to the proper functioning of the Hebraic society in a fundamental way. It was a ritual that brought the child into a covenantal relationship with God and this covenantal relationship had certain rules that were to govern that relationship and these rules also had elements to them that involved what male Jewish believers were going to be expected to do when it came to their sexual lives. The following quote illustrates this point very well:

"This covenant with G-d surpasses human comprehension. It is a bond that pledges unconditional devotion, no matter what may transpire between G-d and individual. It is a bond that is absolute and unchallengeable. For this reason a Jew is circumcised as an infant, when he has not yet developed his capacity for reasoning or making judgements, for the covenant of circumcision is not an intellectual or calculated partnership. The circumcision of an infant demonstrates that the connection between the Jews and G-d is beyond rationale.

G-d chose the very organ that is the source of life, **which can also be chosen to use for the basest acts,** as the site to be sanctified with circumcision. **This gives us the profound message that we can use every physical drive for holy purposes.**"[38]

And what rules governed the sexual behavior of men in the Old Testament period? Many examples are found in the Bible, but the 18th chapter of the book

---

[38] Dovid Zaklikowski - http://www.chabad.org/library/article_cdo/aid/1452224/jewish/Why-Circumcise.htm

of Leviticus goes into great detail about what types of sexual behaviors are not allowed.

What is very interesting is that as has been mentioned here, some of these practices were practiced by Middle Eastern nations (the Egyptians and the Canaanites are mentioned in Leviticus 18:3) and these nations and peoples were strongly condemned by God in the Bible for engaging in these practices.

Now, how do we know that circumcision is linked to the matter of sex and sexual activity? There are several reasons for this. Let us consider this now.

In this regard, let us consider an important commentary on circumcision given by the late Dr. Ernest L. Martin[39], who, in contextualizing the discussion first points out the importance of mankind's relation and place in the physical world, saying:

"Some insist that nature is the creation of God that all humans can enjoy and that the things in nature show forth the finest principles of God's requirements for man's conduct and social activities. After all, as some state: "If God made the natural things the way they are and He said in Genesis that all his creation was 'very good,' then we humans can confidently follow the laws that govern nature in our conduct and social activities."[40]

While the biblical text does mention the following concerning our ability to learn from nature, not only can we learn from nature what *to do*, but we can also learn from nature, what *not to do*. Note Job 12:7-10:

---

[39] The late Dr. Ernest L. Martin was the father of the author of this book. Due to the importance of the work Dr. Martin did on the issue of circumcision, extended excerpts from a newsletter that Dr. Martin published in 1991, which represent the only major resource Dr. Martin ever prepared concerning this subject are referenced in this research study.
[40] Ernest L. Martin, June Communicator: ASK: Portland, OR:1991

"But ask the beasts, and they will teach you; the birds of the heavens, and they will tell you; or the bushes of the earth, and they will teach you; and the fish of the sea will declare to you. Who among all these does not know that the hand of the LORD has done this? In his hand is the life of every living thing and the breath of all mankind." (ESV)

Certainly one can learn from the animals, the plants and from creation, but ultimately mankind is elevated from the creation because he and she are made in the image of God, both male and female, and God has not left us human beings without a divine revelation to help guide our ethics and in particular in this case what men do with their bodies.

"If this is the case, then none of us needs an inspired revelation called "the Holy Scriptures" which often tells us to do the very opposite of what we find the animals, plants and the inanimate objects doing. The truth is, however, mankind needs the biblical revelation which tells us NOT in all cases to act like the animals, plants and the other natural elements." (*ibid.*, Martin.)

Continuing Martin comments:

"Animals, plants and the elements, however, are governed by a very different set of principles. Though Paul said in Romans One that mankind ought to look at the physical creation of God to realize that there is indeed a God who is all-powerful and wise, Paul did not mean for a moment that mankind ought to act like the animals and plants in many things that God has programmed for them to do, or that He allows them to do. In fact, Paul condemned many of the early Romans (and this applies to all races on earth) for abandoning proper principles of conduct that God commanded and they departed into a grossness of wrong living like the animals." (*ibid.* Martin)

Now, the deeper revelation of God to mankind, urges mankind to separate themselves from the animals by the use of their minds and in this case, we are urged to use our minds to learn from God through His Holy Word. This is our standard for our own ethical conduct, not letting nature take its course.

"Those who insist that nature alone is enough of a teacher to guide us in our personal conduct and our social responsibilities to the rest of humanity (and to the rest of creation) are not ones who feel that we need a divine revelation from God to tell us humans how to conduct ourselves. Those who love the Holy Scriptures, however, believe that the instruction book for human conduct is found in the Old and the New Testaments." (*ibid.*)

We have seen some of the earlier explanatory Biblical texts, which show the orientation of the Bible to the issue of the circumcised person or thing compared to uncircumcised person or thing, but now we need to look more into detail at the deep symbolic meaning of circumcision itself and make no mistake that meaning was supernatural and it had a direct link to practices associated with sexual ethics. Martin continues saying:

"From the time of Abraham onward (when the circumcision rite was first inaugurated), the Gentile nations normally ridiculed this ceremony as being unnatural to the way God created us. The principal argument that the Gentiles used was that such a ritual was contrary to nature. Believe me, the Gentiles had a point. To the natural mind, it is better to leave nature alone and keep things the way God created them in the first place. This makes perfectly good sense. But this is the very point that God wanted to impress on Abraham and his descendants who covenanted with God to use this ceremony as the sign that they (the Jews) were God's covenant people." (*ibid.* Martin)

The fact that all boys were born with their foreskins intact according to nature's design is an important one. What circumcision teaches us is that those who receive it were not going to be "natural oriented" men. That is right! They were going to be supernatural! They were going to become a holy nation, a priestly people (Exodus 19:6) and they were. This is because from the time that they received this personal sign in their bodies, their families and their entire communities were making a commitment to raise them according to the rules laid down in the Law of God. Martin comments on this fact saying:

"Look with what all male children are born. Jewish boy babies as well as all Gentile baby boys are born as nature intended with the foreskin intact. That is what nature intended. Then God came along and commanded the father to make the Jewish boy different from all other male children. The father was commanded to go against nature and cut off that foreskin of his boy on his eighth day of life. This sign was to show the boy and his parents [and the society in which they lived] that he was to be different from what the codes and principles of nature showed was natural. Indeed, this boy was to be different from what nature intended. This was the very point God was making with Abraham and his descendants. The very fact that a part of their physical anatomy had been cut off to make them different showed that God did not expect them to act like natural human beings. This made each Jewish boy in covenant relationship with God, and God expected each of them to act in conformity to that relationship. In other words, the Jewish boys

57

were from then on constantly reminded not to let "Nature Take its Course," because they were no longer to be like those who kept only the laws of nature as their guidelines. It was the Gentiles who relied on the religion of nature and most of their holydays[41] were centered around the seasons of nature." (*ibid.* Martin)

Now, the fact that the circumcision procedure was undertaken on the male organ for procreation is important. It is not accidental. It has a specific purpose in mind when this particular organ was chosen for this most holy of rituals and once again it is essential to reiterate that this procedure was done to the infant child and it was known by his family and also by his community because it was undertaken with normally ten male witnesses. By taking part in this ritual, the child was entering into a holy community which had sexual ethical standards defined by God and this ritual reinforced those sexual ethical standards which all were expected to accept and obey. Further Martin comments on this point saying:

"This meant that a Jewish boy and Jewish man every time he took hold of that part of the anatomy in the middle part of his body (which usually occurred on a daily basis for natural reasons) was to remind him that he was different than all other men. He was a unique person who was in covenant relationship with God Almighty while others were not. The Jew was to be an unnatural man. He was instead to be a man motivated by spiritual principles.

---

[41] Everything about the behavior, conduct and lifestyle of that child was going to be different. Note even the days of worship that the Jewish people had were in some cases unnatural in their orientation. While Gentiles worshipped the seasonal days according to the orientation of the moon and the seasons, the Jewish people had an unnatural day, which God had given them, the Sabbath, to be their weekly holyday. The Sabbath has no astronomical phenomena that helps in determining it. It is a day which was pronounced and made holy by God and it has nothing to do with natural phenomena. The same thing could be said for the Sabbatical Years, a key seven-year calendrical feature of the Bible in which the land of Israel was to lie fallow and uncultivated. This seven-year cycle is also unnatural according to astronomical phenomena.

In other words, the physical difference of the Jew through circumcision was to reflect the Jew's spiritual difference in every aspect of his life. Every day when the natural functions of the body became manifest, the Jewish man in the exercise of those physical factors was reminded that he was different. He was to be a representative of God and to be kind, considerate and loving to others. He was reminded not to be like a natural man who often conducted himself like the beasts of the field. The Jew was to show forth the faithfulness of God and a respect to all mankind. He was to remind the Gentiles of God's faithfulness to them through His covenant with Noah. The Jew was also to be like God who was forgiving and comforting to mankind in their lives. In a word, the fact of circumcision made the Jew different from all other men. They were not the natural sort of man that almost all other people were. They were God's people." (*ibid.* Martin)

God's people also were expected to agree to and keep certain ethical rules for their conduct and this was especially the case for the human male of the species who was singled out for receiving the physical sign of circumcision. To conclude on this point, Dr. Martin said:

"The point of circumcision is that it was on the generative organ of the man -- the place where all human life comes from. In actual fact, all life comes from God himself, but the part of the human anatomy that illustrates this is the male organ. The symbol was to be reckoned in a holy sense by the Jewish man and it was not to be looked on as being crass and degrading. The circumcision covenant was made on the organ that gave life to mankind and it was intended to remind Jewish men not simply of sex or sexual pleasure, but of God who gives life to all.

Gentile people often viewed such symbolism as absurd and they sometimes made crass remarks about this spiritual characteristic that accompanied the Jewish men. It is better not to make levity of such things, because I do not think our heavenly Father and Christ Jesus would be pleased with such things." (*ibid.*)

Finally, Dr. Martin mentioned the following to conclude this thought:

"Circumcision was to remind Jewish men that they should always use that part of their anatomy in agreement with their covenant relationship with God that they have. The strongest emotions and desires of mankind often center around this part of the anatomy. Even manliness and machismoism can be associated with its function. And there was to be nothing restricted in its use as long as what was done was in conformity to the laws of God's covenant." (*ibid.*)

Understanding the other barriers that protected the holiness of circumcised boys or men

As we have mentioned herein, circumcised men and boys were in a special covenant relationship with God, but God also understood that human beings were weak and could be tempted to engage in sinful behavior of a sexual nature. This is where additional laws that applied to men only were created to help put additional personal physical barriers between the individual and the possibility that person would commit unlawful sexual acts.

5.   Circumcision:

Its Link to Clothing, Fringes, Phylacteries, Barriers and Privacy

In discussing the issue of circumcision and its link to the acknowledgement, necessity and promotion for the believer in God to lead a holy life and to think about what he does with his own body, the issue of clothing, privacy, sanctification and the commandments of God enter the conversation.

The fact is, there is a direct link between the commandment of circumcision as well as certain commandments only for men which required them to wear certain articles of clothing which were absolutely linked to helping them remember to lead sanctified lives. The role of these items is understood as follows:

"Man is composed of flesh and blood and, as such, he is subject to many sensual lusts; be he also possesses an opposing force – his soul. The soul deters him from engaging solely in the pursuit of the pleasures of the flesh. The soul, emanating from heaven, is operating for from its base when it is dealing with earthly lusts. Hence it sometimes becomes weak and ineffective and the lists of the body overcome the prudence of the soul, with the result that the soul requires assistance."[42]

The clothing that we wear says something about us. This was definitely the case in ancient times and the believers in the one true creator of heaven and earth had certain requirements concerning that they had to adhere to. These requirements had a meaning and which helped support their pursuit of godliness and holiness.

Clothing has a supporting role in that it helps to secure the privacy of an individual. Certain matters of the physical body are private and are designed to be

---

[42] Chill, The Mitzvot: The Commandments & their Rationale: Keter Books: Jerusalem,1974, 378

that way by God. This is the case for men and women. Having said that, the Bible indicates that there were additional legal requirements for men in this area.

The Vision of the Resurrected Jesus Christ in the Book of Revelation

To start this discussion, let us look at a heavenly description of our Lord Jesus Christ because this description can instruct us in some very interesting points about how Christ chooses to attire Himself at the present time. Look at it here:

"Then I turned to see the voice that was speaking to me, and on turning I saw seven golden lampstands, and in the midst of the lampstands one like a son of man, **clothed with a long robe** and with a golden sash around his chest. The hairs of his head were white, like white wool, like snow. His eyes were like a flame of fire, his feet were like burnished bronze, refined in a furnace, and his voice was like the roar of many waters. In his right hand he held seven stars, from his mouth came a sharp two-edged sword, and his face was like the sun shining in full strength. When I saw him, I fell at his feet as though dead. But he laid his right hand on me, saying, "Fear not, I am the first and the last, and the living one. I died, and behold I am alive forevermore, and I have the keys of Death and Hades." (Revelation 1:12-18 ESV)

In looking at the original Greek of v. 13, we note that this "long robe" was one which "reached to the feet", yet as v.15 shows us, 'his feet" were visible to Saint John because he described them.

Now, I think that most Christians would agree that our Lord Jesus Christ is a being in his personal example in everything He does is one who exhibits holiness and is one to be emulated. This is especially the case in regard to matters of dress and I think that what we have here in Revelation can be instructive to us.

The Role of Clothing and Its Connection to the
Issue of Personal Holiness for Human Beings

Now, I think that most people will agree that a person who would dress today like the example of the Lord Jesus and His picture here in the book of Revelation will have to admit that this type of description exhibits a type of clothing that is holier than some other types of clothing that a male could wear.

For example, this description would have to be considered holier than a robe on a man that reached say mid-thigh. In addition, were a man to be wearing trousers compared to a full-length robe to the feet, I think that most people would agree that the long robe would exhibit more holiness due to the fact that the bodily features are not as easily evident on someone who is wearing the robe.

Taking the example further, were a man to be wearing short pants, I think that people could say in general that short trousers would exhibit a less holy appearance overall than long trousers and certainly a less holy appearance than a male wearing a long robe which reached to the feet.

Now, why are we discussing this matter of clothing and holiness anyway especially in a context dealing with the issue of circumcision? This is because there is a direct connection between the teaching of circumcision to additional teachings in the Hebrew Bible in particular, which are linked to various articles of clothing and their role in enhancing the holy status of the human male in particular. As circumcision had a role in reminding the person who received it to be holy, it also had a role in helping support the ongoing sanctified behavior of the individual in question and the direction that the circumcised person took in their lives, namely to be pure and holy in matters related to sexuality and to move towards marriage and having children who would be raised up in the same way.

Some general information about male clothing in the Biblical Period

The Bible speaks about clothing for men (which is our focus) with the following historical facts. We are here not covering every item of clothing as mentioned in the Bible, but rather only those pieces of clothing which are relevant to our present circumcision discussion:

1.   "The *shirt* (or *tunic*) in Hebrew (כתנת – *kitto'neth*) ... It was the usual under-garment[43] of youths[44] and men[45], also of the priests and Levites in their service.[46] Female tunics or "*chemises*" were also called by the same name.[47] The *kittoneth* was commonly quite short, scarcely reaching to the knee;"[48]

2.   "but eventually, as a peculiar kind, there is mentioned[49] as an ornamental dress of young persons of either sex, the *kittoneth passim'*, כתנת פסים, *tunic of the extremities*, i.e. reaching to the feet (for so the word appears to signify;[50]; rather than *party-colored tunic*, 'coat of many colors,"[51]), which was an under-dress with sleeves and extending to the ankles.[52]" (*ibid.*)

3.   "The *mantle* or *robe*, a comprehensive term that appears to include several Hebrew words, signifying not only a long-flowing outer garment, but sometimes

---

[43] Compare Leviticus16:4
[44] Genesis 27:3, 23, etc.
[45] II Samuel 15:32
[46] Exodus 28:40; Leviticus 8:7, 13; 10:5
[47] II Samuel 13:18; Song of Songs 5:3
[48] CBTEL, vol. I, pg.529
[49] Genesis 23:32; 27:3; II Samuel 13:18 sq.
[50] See Gesenius *Thes. Heb.* p. 1117
[51] As in the Authorized Version after the Septuagint and Vulgate
[52] Josephus, Antiquities, 7.8.1

also a wide under-garment or double tunic. It sometimes approaches the signific-ation of "veil" (see below), as this was often like a modern cloak, or at least shawl. Ewald separates the word thus: פתי גיל (*pethi gil*), *breadth of mantle* (compare Syr. גולתא). In the New Testament, the mantle is denoted by στολή (Greek: *stole*), a robe, such as the scribes wore[53], a long garment like a gown, reaching to the feet.

4.   The girdle, in Hebrew חגור, *chagor'*, or חגורה, *chagorah'* (the usual name for male and female girdles,[54]); one of the most distinguished articles of attire among the Hebrews and Orientals[55], being a belt by which the under-garment (tunic) was gathered at the waist, and thus prevented from floating, as well as hindering the person in walking[56] or in any other bodily motions[57]. Hence, girdles were often bestowed as presents[58], and were an article of fancy goods[59]. The poor and ascetic cases wore girdles of leather[60], the rich, linen[61] or byssus (sea silk)[62]; the moderns even of silk, of some four fingers' breadth,[63], ornamented[64]; a Persian fashion,[65] in a costly manner (with gold, jewels); this last description was especially valued in female girdles, which, being an indispensable part of household manufacture.[66]

5.   The men wore girdles about the loins[67] but priests wore them somewhat higher around the breast[68] - men's girdles were generally called אזור *ezor'."* (*ibid.*)

---

[53] Mark 12:38
[54] Isaiah 3:24
[55] Compare Ezekiel 23:15; Daniel 10:5
[56] I Kings 18:46; I Kings 4:29; 9:1
[57] Sometimes dancing, II Samuel 6:14
[58] II Samuel 18:11; I Maccabees 10:87
[59] Proverbs 31:24
[60] II Kings 1:8; Matthew 3:4; Mark 1:6, as they still do in the East, of half a foot in width
[61] Jeremiah 13:1; compare Arieux, iii.247
[62] Ezekiel 16:10
[63] Mariti, p. 214; Chardin, iii.68
[64] Daniel 10:5; I Maccabees 10:89; 11:58; 14:44; Curt. iii., 3, 18; compare Arvieux, iii.241
[65] Xenophon. Anab. 1,4,9; compare Brisson, Regn. Pers. p.169 sq.
[66] Proverbs 31:17
[67] II Kings 4:29; Jeremiah 13:11; Revelation 1:13;
[68] Josephus, Antiquities, iii.7.2

Four Cornered Garments and
their Importance to Human Males Within Judaism

As we are showing in this research study, there is a strong link between the issue of circumcision and the issue of male clothing. This is because the Jewish male was commanded by God to wear certain articles of clothing and that matter was not a question of maybe or perhaps. No! It was a command of All Mighty God which was expected to be taken seriously and to be kept. This command, known in Hebrew as a *mitzvah* (a commandment) was one of 613 such commandments that Jewish believers were required to keep as a part of their service to God.

The Middle Age Rabbinical Scholar Maimonides sums up the rationale for keeping these commandments saying:

"The mitzvah, according to Maimonides, acts as a prophylactic against the onslaughts of the *yetzer ha ra* – 'man's evil inclination." (Chill, pg. xiii)

Hadai Crescas viewed the *mitzvoth* (plural of *mitzvah*) as instruments designed to bind the Jew to his God and foster the love and the fear of Him." (*ibid.*)

Now, of the 613 mitzvot (commandments), many are considered very important, but, in fact, this commandment to wear a four cornered garment which had "Tzitzit" (fringes) on the four corners is one of the most important in all of the Torah. Note Rabbi Chill once again:

"The *mitzvah* of *tzitzit* is consider one the most important of all the mitzvot. The Rabbis equate this one mitzvah with the rest of the 613. First, the Torah itself hints at its importance when it says: 'When you shall see it, you shall remember all the mitzvot." (*ibid.* quoting Numbers 15:38-40)

This text from Num. 15: 38-40 is a very important one and must be quoted here:

"Speak to the children of Israel, and say to them that they shall make for themselves fringes on the corners of their garments, throughout their generations, and that they shall affix a thread of sky-blue [wool] on the fringe of each corner. This shall be tzitzit [fringes] for you, and when you see it, you will remember all the commandments of God to perform them, and you shall not wander after your hearts and after your eyes after which you are going astray. So that you shall remember and perform all My commandments, and you shall be holy to your Lord."

This text is a most important Scripture. This is because these fringes on the garment were meant to remind the wearer, who was a believing Jewish male (tzitzit were not worn by women), in particular of his need to pursue a holy and consecrated life.

When you think about this issue in a practical sense, you can see the very real possibility of how this garment played a role to constantly remind the God fearing Jewish man of the important to "be consecrated to your God" (v.40), "you will remember all the commands of the LORD" (v.38), and "not to follow after your own heart and your own eyes which you are inclined to whore after." (v.39)

We can see in this text the holiness that these fringes on the garment were designed to help the men to remember their obligations and responsibilities to God under the Law of Moses. Let us further consider the rationale for this:

"The *mitzvah* of *tzitzit* is considered one of the most important of all the *mitzvot*. The Rabbis equate this one *mitzvah* with the rest of the 613. First, the Torah itself hints at its importance when it says: 'When you shall see it, you shall remember all the mitzvot.' … The Rabbis taught that God punishes those who avoid waring garments that require fringes to escape the obligation. It is therefore customary to wear a garment with *tzitziyyot* continually." (*ibid.*, Chill, pg. 339)

Further commentators point out the importance of this religious requirement:

"Hizzekuni: He reasons that when one looks at the fringes of this garment, which remind him of God's mitzvot, he will bear in mind that he is God's servant and that his heart and eye must not be led astray." (*ibid.* pg. 340)

"Man requires a constant reminder that he is expected to observe the mitzvot. Through the ever-present fringes of this garment, it is hope that the time will come when he will be thinking of the mitzvot all the time. The purpose of the reminder is to help the wearer to lead a holy life and this conduct should eventually become natural to him." (*ibid.*)

Phylacteries: An additional layer of clothing supporting a holy life

We have mentioned how circumcision was considered a "sign" (Hebrew: אות) in the flesh to the one who undertook the procedure. Now, in regard to clothing or adornment, there is another concept which is also termed a "sign" and its practice is linked to holiness. This concerns the biblical requirement for men to wear phylacteries (Hebrew: תפילין – *tefillin*)

Phylacteries are a requirement of the Law of Moses (Deut. 6:8) as follows:

"Bind them as a sign on your hand, fix them as an emblem on your forehead,"

We note above the English word "sign", which is the same word used to describe circumcision as we have mentioned. This is important. Note the following:

"There are certain rituals which are referred to in the Torah as an "Ot" – a sign of the binding relationship between the Jew and God. The Sabbath is called an "Ot"; circumcision is described as an "Ot"; the *mitzvah* of *tefillin* joins the group of "Otot." (plural for "Ot.") (Chill, pg. 379)

First, Phylacteries were only worn by men and only during the day:

"*Tefillin* are worn only during the day. Since there is a time element involved, it is not incumbent upon the woman to fulfill this *mitzvah*." (*ibid.*)

Phylacteries were not legally required at night when the young man was already at home and moving towards the time of daily sleep.

Next, Phylacteries were worn by men starting at 13, the Bar Mitzvah age:

"In some oriental communities, the climax of the celebration (of Bar Mitzvah) is the first wearing of the phylacteries."[69]

It is logical that phylacteries would become binding around age 13. This is the normal time when young men become physically mature and normal physical desires start to be more relevant to the mind and the bodies of young men change.

---

[69] Roth, Cecil, The Standard Jewish Encyclopedia, Doubleday & Co.: New York, 1959, p. 234

This is when phylacteries become a legal requirement for the young believer. They support the young man in his pursuit of living a holy lifestyle:

"One of the guardians of the soul in its battle with the body is the mitzvah of tefillin. By wearing tefillin we help to tip the scale in favor of the soul."[70]

Phylacteries direct the attention of the wearer to the thoughts of their minds and the works of their hands seeking to direct the wearer towards a holy life:

"By wearing the tefillin on the arm and the head, indicating that the work of our hands and the thoughts of our brains must be dedicated to God, we have a constant reminder not to follow the dictates of evil inclination." (*ibid.* pg. 378-9)

So, in addition to the other clothing items mentioned earlier, as a young man grew up, a new level of spiritual support to pursue a holy life became a daily part of his life and reality. This was another outward sign that he was different, was sanctified and as such was supposed to live a holy life focusing his attention on God.

As Dr. Martin mentioned about the role of circumcision, which reminded the Jewish male that he was different than other people and a holy person. But, as the human male would on a daily basis take hold of the middle part of his anatomy for normal bodily functions, his physical state of circumcision and his clothing provided him a constant reminder or even a "prophylactic against the onslaught of the *'yetzer ha-ra'*" (Hebrew: יֵצֶר הָרַע) (man's evil inclination) (*ibid.*)

---

[70] "Man is composed of flesh and blood and, as such, he is subject to many sensual lusts; be he also possesses an opposing force – his soul. The soul deters him from engaging solely in the pursuit of the pleasures of the flesh. The soul, emanating from heaven, is operating for from its base when it is dealing with earthly lusts. Hence it sometimes becomes weak and ineffective and the lists of the body over-come the prudence of the soul, with the result that the soul requires assistance. One of the guardians of the soul in its battle with the body is the mitzvah of tefillin. By wearing tefillin we help to tip the scale in favor of the soul." (Chill, pg. 378)

Here we have to understand practically that for a man to engage in and commit sexual sin, first he must decide in his mind to commit sin. That is the first step, but after that he would have to remove his phylacteries and then his girdle and outer garment (the robe or mantle noted earlier) that had the fringes. First, regarding the girdle, we are often reminded in Scripture that men are urged to:

"gird one's self" or "gird up your loins" or "gird up your loins like a man.[71]

These phrases are used of grown men urging them to be mature or prepared and act like a mature man. The girdle would have been the first item of direct clothing that had to be removed to undertake sin of a sexual nature. So, we have a primary reminder of God's law. Then we would remove the robe, which had the fringes which were a direct reminder of the Law of God. Then, he would need to remove an additional garment which was worn next to the skin (this was the tunic). At this point, the man would be naked, which as we know from Scripture was a state which was reserved only for holy and sanctified activities on the part of grown men.[72] Then, the man would encounter the final reminder beyond just being physically naked, which would be his physical circumcised state.

This also reminds us in a way of how God thinks about the need to protect ourselves from doing things that could cause either ourselves or others to sin or be harmed. Here the text in Deuteronomy 22:8 about making a fence around the roof of your house comes to mind. This idea of building protection around the roof of your house so someone does not fall are often extended to other areas of the life of the believer. Here we can see the same idea with the ritual of circumcision and the holy garments that have these fringes. The holy

---

[71] Isa. 8:9; Psa. 86:11; I Kgs 18:46; II Kgs 4:29; 9:1; Job 38:3; 40:7; Jere. 1:17; Nahum 2:1
[72] Genesis 9:22,23

garments acted like a fence (as we have mentioned earlier, a type of protection) around the human being, in this case the male human being, to protect him against sin and its negative results.

Circumcision and Barriers:
To Avoid Sin, Build Fences Around Fences Around Fences

What we see in this discussion is that God is building fences around the human being even reaching down to the very physical body of the person. This is just how important this whole matter is. In this regard, we can also learn something from further teachings about the need to put barriers around situations to protect and save life.

One of these concerns the teaching called "Khumra." Note Wikipedia:

"1. A khumra (חומרה; pl. חומרות, khumrot) is a prohibition or obligation in Jewish practice that exceeds the bare requirements of Jewish law. One who imposes a khumra on him- or herself in a given instance is said to be מחמיר makhmir. The rationale for a khumra comes from Deuteronomy 22:8, which states that when one builds a house, he must build a fence around the roof in order to avoid guilt should someone fall off the roof. This has been interpreted by many as a requirement to "build a fence around the Torah" in order to protect the mitzvot."

An obligation or prohibition can be adopted by an individual or an entire community. Early references to khumrot are found in the Talmud, and the understanding and application of them has changed over time.

Most often found in Orthodox Judaism, khumrot are variously seen as a precaution against transgressing the Halakha or as a way of keeping those who have taken on the stringency separate from those who have not.

This definition to someone who has never heard of this idea might be a bit hard to understand. I understand this teaching like this.

For example, in the Bible, a person was not permitted to eat a fish that did not have fins and scales. Now, for those seeking to meet these requirements in a more stringent way, they might propose additional prohibitions or obligations to ensure that one does not eat a fish that is considered unclean and not allowed. This is the idea we are talking about.

So what could a person do to avoid eating such a fish? First, to eat something, you have to touch it. So, another level would be: You are not allowed to touch an unclean fish.

Now, depending on the circumstances that a person found around him or herself, one could even extend a prohibition to a greater level. How might this happen? One could say: "To ensure that I don't touch a fish that is unclean (because I am not allowed to eat), I am not going to enter a fish shop that sells non-kosher fish.

Now, this might seem extreme and I guess from one point of view, it might be, but one also might also think about the circumstances one finds oneself in, where such prohibitions might even be helpful. We could even extend this idea to say that to avoid eating a fish, not only will not touch such a fish and not enter a place where such fish are sold and I might also extend the prohibition to include not even frequenting a street where the shop that sells such fish is located.

Now, I personally believe that we have the roots of such ideas even in the Bible. It is not to evident to those who are unfamiliar with this idea, but after becoming more familiar with this idea, you start to see it popping up in the Biblical texts in a way which seems to point towards its relevance. Note the following text which could be interpreted quite easily in this fashion.

"Hear, my son, your father's instruction, and forsake not your mother's teaching, for they are a graceful garland for your head and pendants for your neck. My son, if sinners entice you, do not consent. If they say, "Come with us, let us lie in wait for blood; let us ambush the innocent without reason;…" (Proverbs 1:8-11 ESV)

Now, in looking at this text in light of the idea of building a fence around a fence around a fence, you can see here what these parents are telling their son. They are telling him "If evil people ask you to join with them, say 'No'." Then, note the next level we find in this text. It says: "Come with us…" This is a new level, because the parent knows that the child may not be able to resist the first level. That first fence around the sinful thing might not be enough. So the advice given is of a greater intensity or a higher level. Look at it!

It says just after this: "my son, do not walk in the way with them; hold back your foot from their paths, (Proverbs 1:15 ESV)

This is totally a new level! To avoid sin by hurting someone, first you say no, but if you still feel tempted, don't hang out with these people!

Now, what about another level? Think about this. Here is another text to consider in this idea of building fences around fences around fences. Let us review it now. We have some discussion in the Scriptures about sin which takes places outside of the home. (Proverbs 7:10-11; I Timothy 5:13; Titus 2:5) Note also an exceedingly important text from the book of Isaiah:

"Come, my people, enter your chambers, and shut your doors behind you; hide yourselves for a little while until the fury has passed by." (Isaiah 26:20 ESV)

What we find in these texts is an additional prohibition of even exiting a house to avoid evil. This is exactly what is being taught in these texts. One could create a formulation that looks like this.

1.   To avoid sin if people were asking me engage in sinful behavior, I would refuse

2.   To ensure that I refuse from engaging in sinful behavior that some might ask me to engage in, I would avoid frequenting places where such people congregate.

3.   To further ensure that I do not engage in sinful behavior, which some might ask me to engage in, not only will I not visit places where they might frequent, to ensure that this does not happen, I will remain in my own home!

This is how I understand this issue of prohibition from behaviors which could lead one to sin. This is hard place to find oneself, but we even find this discussed in the book of Proverbs and it tells us what to do. Note Proverbs 6:1-10:

"My son, if you have put up security for your neighbor, have given your pledge for a stranger, if you are snared in the words of your mouth, caught in the words of your mouth, then do this, my son, and save yourself, for you have come into the hand of your neighbor: go, hasten, and plead urgently with your neighbor. Give your eyes no sleep and your eyelids no slumber; save yourself like a gazelle from the hand of the hunter, like a bird from the hand of the fowler. Go to the ant, O sluggard; consider her ways, and be wise. Without having any chief, officer, or ruler, she prepares her bread in summer and gathers her food in harvest. How long will you lie there, O sluggard? When will you arise from your sleep? A little sleep, a little slumber, a little folding of the hands to rest. (ESV)

You can see the levels here. If you find yourself in an environment where you feel you are not right with God or in sin, run the other way; go to the person who is holding this sway over you and get out of the situation; Don't rest until you have removed yourself; Be like an animal running away from someone trying to trap it.

In conclusion, we can see that the teaching of circumcision and other teachings we have herein referenced are very much linked to focusing on living a holy life. The final comment from Dr. Martin sums this up saying:

"The teaching of the Scriptures is that we all should be trying to live above our natural inclinations; that we should be different from all other humans; and that our emphasis should mostly be on spiritual matters."[73]

Circumcision and Privacy:
God is a Being who demands Privacy as should Humankind

The final point in our discussion about circumcision here concerns the private nature of the practice. Circumcision takes place on the male organ of reproduction which under normal circumstances is private and governed by social laws where such parts of the body are generally under normal circumstances kept private. There is some theological teaching to be learned regarding this point:

---

[73] Ernest L. Martin, June Communicator: ASK: Portland, OR:1991

"The second point of circumcision was the fact that it was made in a part of the body which was normally secret and private. Only the Jewish boy, his parents and other Jews knew he was circumcised in a physical sense. This meant that the Jewish man had to show others he was truly circumcised not by showing them that part of his anatomy, but by his actions and his spiritual way of life. This meant that the Jew was not to be outwardly religious in a physical or ritualistic way, but that he would not boast of his covenant relationship with God (that others did not have), but that he would render his services to God and man in a private and non-ostentatious manner."[74]

This issue of privacy in religious matters reflects something very much linked to how God operates in His relations with mankind. God wants privacy. He also understands and respects our personal privacy.

God is a being who demands privacy. Note the following quote from Dr. Martin in this regard:

"Does He [God] have and demand privacy? The answer is "yes." ... For one, God and Christ are always depicted as having clothes on their bodies. Such garments would not be necessary for protection from the heat of the sun or the cold of winter, but clothes are used for other important reasons. They provide a decoration (that is, beauty of dress), for an insignia of rank, and most important to our present discussion, for privacy. Not only that, the Temple at Jerusalem was an exact pattern of God's home (his palace) in heaven (Hebrews 9:23), and in that Temple were three main compartments in which God's own people (the ones He loved the most) could come into His presence. Only in the outer court could Israelites appear. In the inner court, only priests were allowed. But into the Holy

---

[74] *ibid.*

of Holies, only the High Priest could come into that region, and then only once a year on the Day of Atonement. That inner region represented God's dwelling place and where His throne was situated. Only at designated times could those whom God loved enter into His presence. This means that God demands a certain privacy and respect regarding the dignity of His person. Also, even the angels of God could only appear before Him at certain times and all of those times were when the angels were invited to do so (see Job 1:6; 2:1)."[75]

The teaching of circumcision has a very strong linkage to personal privacy. It concerns personal and private matters. But there is one thing about the teaching of circumcision which is not linked to privacy. It is something which originally took place in private, but the outcome of circumcision is very much connected to what takes place in the public sphere motivated by actions of the inward man. St. Paul called upon Christians to have a circumcision "of the heart" saying:

"The apostle Paul told the Roman Gentiles that all Christians (male or female) should be Jews inwardly. "For he is not a Jew which is one outwardly; neither is that circumcision which is outward in the flesh; but he is a Jew which is one inwardly; and circumcision is that of the heart, in the spirit and not in the letter; whose praise is not of men, but of God. (Romans 2:28,29)"[76].

While God respects our privacy, He expects us to operate in the public sphere in a way that He wishes motivated by the Holy Spirit of God. This is what circumcision is all about: a change of heart towards right living.

---

[75] Ernest L. Martin, "What will life be like beyond the Resurrection?" ASK: Portland, OR: 1995.
[76] Ernest L. Martin, June Communicator: ASK: Portland, OR:1991

6. Circumcision: Why was it done at such an early age?

One of the hardest things to understand about circumcision was why it was done on boys who were just born and only eight days old. I mean an infant of that age is so small and so tender, how could the LORD ever recommend such a thing to be done? This is the question all of us ask and want to have the answer.

The first thing we have to do to really start down the road to answering this question is to put aside all of our biases and emotions. We need to have a practical academic reason what is taking place concerning this being done on boys who are according to the Law of Moses are to be circumcised on the eighth day of life.

What we also have to do is project ourselves back in time to really see what was taking place not from our perspective today, but what was taking place in the society that caused the LORD to introduce this practice. Rest assured, what was taking place was so horrifying that circumcision was introduced to combat and protect the boy children being born at that time. This may seem like a fantastic statement, but this is the exact teaching that we find in the Bible.

The thing that we first need to understand is that God loves His creation and His children are the most important part of that creation. God is the perfect exponent of Love. (God would never give something to mankind which did not have their best interests in His heart. If we believe this, then we are on the right road to understanding the rationale for circumcision.

God gives His Signs to Mankind to Protect Them

One of the important teachings that we find in Genesis prior to the time that circumcision (which we have already identified as an external sign for boy babies)

79

was introduced, involved another sign of an external nature given to another male individual in Genesis. Who was this and what were the circumstances?

The "Mark" That Was Given to Cain Was a "Sign" For Cain's Protection

It is not apparent in most English versions of the Bible, but an important point must be raised concerning Cain[77] and the mark that he was given by the LORD. Cain was given this mark to protect him from being killed. Cain was certainly afraid of being killed for what he had done. (Genesis 4:14)

The problem is in the English translation of the word "mark", because in the Hebrew original, this word, "mark" is the same exact word used to describe the circumcision covenant. In Hebrew is it "*ohth*." (אות) In Genesis 17:11, it is often translated as "token", but in Hebrew it is exactly the same. We see in the first instance where this word appears in Scripture (Genesis 1:14), it is translated as "sign" (in this case in the plural – signs) and it concerns the fact that the LORD gave the heavenly bodies to mankind "for signs and for seasons" (*ibid.*)

What we find is that in the first instances describing the things that the LORD gave to mankind as "signs", these were things that were good for mankind. Note them:

- The sun and the moon and the stars (Genesis 1:14)
- The mark that protected Cain from being killed (Genesis 4:15)
- The rainbow (Genesis 9:12,13,17)
- Circumcision (Genesis 17:11)

---

[77] For more information on this subject, see my work "What was the Mark of Cain?" – Available here https://www.amazon.com/gp/product/B08ZVNBT54/ref=dbs_a_def_rwt_bibl_vppi_i0

The thing we want to pay attention to in regard to the first two instances where this word is used regarding human beings (Cain and Abraham), there is an element of protection involved concerning giving them these "signs."

It is obvious what the protection the LORD gave to Cain was. It was to protect his life from being killed by someone who might take revenge on him for killing his brother. What is important for us to understand though is that circumcision was also given as a "sign of protection" for a boy baby who had entered the covenant of God through receiving the sign of that covenant.

This fact is known to scholars who point out that certain practices, of which circumcision was one, had the goal to preserve human life as one of its rationales.

"In religious history **circumcision** may be seen as a substitute for human sacrifice."[78]

Under the heading, "*Modifications and substitutes for human sacrifice*", we also find the following assertion in Hastings Encyc. Of Rel. and Ethics (see note 44) saying:

"Although, as the notorious case of the Aztecs shows, the practice of human sacrifice is not inconsistent with a high standard of culture, **it is natural that the advance of civilization should develop a repugnance against the rite** [the rite under discussion in this article is human sacrifice] in its crudest form, and that **various devices should be invented to satisfy the demands of the gods without actually taking life**. ... Probably mutilation and similar irreparable injuries – especially those involving the loss of male virility or female chastity – **were devices to preserve life ...**" (vol. VI, pg. 864)

---

[78] https://en.intactiwiki.org/index.php/Circumcision - article « Circumcision »

What did boy babies need protection from in ancient times?

We have pointed out what type of society was developing in the world in the time of Noah. The Bible paints a very grim picture:

"The LORD saw that the wickedness of man was great in the earth, and that every intention of the thoughts of his heart was only evil continually. And the LORD regretted that he had made man on the earth, and it grieved him to his heart." (Genesis 6:5-6 ESV)

This situation lead up to the great cataclysm (Great Flood), which saw the limited civilization wiped out and then recreated also in the physical sense. (Psa. 104:30)

After the great cataclysm, human beings began to multiply and as we are noting in this book, the incident of the Tower of Confusion (Babel) took place in the plains of Mesopotamia. From there civilization began to develop and it was into this environment that the practice of circumcision was introduced.

Now, how does this matter compare with Greco-Roman and Ancient Near Eastern (ANE) culture? From the viewpoint of ANE culture, this text is very mild in comparison. Why? This is because the unholy, murderous barbaric brutality which was associated with some of the ANE beliefs. In particular, we must draw attention to the religious practices associated with the worship of certain Eastern deities which was heinous for the horrific practices which took the lives of boys and girls by the hands of their own parents. These practices are mentioned in the Bible with extreme condemnation by the LORD on numerous occasions. An important text which we need to draw our attention to is found in Deuteronomy 12. This text describes the religious practices of peoples who were living in the land of Israel at the time that Israel entered the Promised Land. We find the LORD demanding that these practices and the places where they were undertaken to be completely obliterated and blotted out. What those ancient nations were doing with their children was barbaric, evil and wrong and it was linked to false religious practices and the LORD tells His people to have nothing to do with these practices.

"You must demolish completely all the places where the nations whom you are about to dispossess served their gods, on the mountain heights, on the hills, and under every leafy tree. Break down their altars, smash their pillars, burn their sacred poles with fire, and hew down the idols of their gods, and thus blot out their name from their places. You shall not worship the Lord your God in such ways." (Deuteronomy 12:2-4 NRSV)

What were some of the practices that these peoples were engaging in relative to their children that were not to be imitated in any way shape or form? Note Deut. 12:29-32:

"When the Lord your God has cut off before you the nations whom you are about to enter to dispossess them, when you have dispossessed them and live in their land, take care that you are not snared into imitating them, after they have been destroyed before you: do not inquire concerning their gods, saying, "How did these nations worship their gods? I also want to do the same." You must not do the same for the Lord your God, because every abhorrent thing that the Lord hates they have done for their gods. They would even burn their sons and their daughters in the fire to their gods. You must diligently observe everything that I command you; do not add to it or take anything from it." (NRSV)

The Israelite peoples were commanded not to do the things that these nations were doing, which as we can see here was horrifying and almost beyond the imagination. **It is in this context that we must see the practice of circumcision introduced.**

Let us also not think that these practices were isolated ones just found in one country. In no way is this true. These practices were widespread all over the Near East:

"Diodorus Siculus (i.88) speaks of the king of Egypt as having formerly sacrificed men of red colour – the colour of Set or Typhon – at the grave of Osiris; and he adds the important details that, as red men were rare in Egypt, the victims were always foreigners."[79]

"From another fragment (*ib. ii.*616, no. 84) it appears that in those or similar sacrifices the victims were 'Typhonic' (= red) men, and were burnt alive." (*ibid.*)

"Procopius (*de. Bell. Pers.* i.19) states that in the temple of Philo the Blemmyes offered human victims to the sun." (*ibid.*)

"Further, the special circumstances of Egypt, dependent on for its life on the Nile inundations, demanded a Nile sacrifice, which the Arab historian Murtadha describes as lasting down to the Muslim occupation of Egypt (A.D. 642) – a young girl being annually cast into the river to ensure a sufficient rise in the water ..." (*ibid.*)

---

[79] Hastings, J.; Encyclopedia of Religion & Ethics, T & T Clark; Edinburgh, 1913. vol. 6, p. 862

Another Bible example of what we are here talking about is mentioned in II Chron. 28:

"But the most remarkable passage is that in 2 Chronicles XXVIII:3, in which the wickedness of Ahaz is described: 'Moveover, he burned incense in the valley of the sons of Hinnom, and burned (וַיַּבְעֵר) his children in the fire, after the abominations of the nations whom Jehovah had driven out before the children of Israel.'"[80]

We have further Scriptural references to these purely evil practices in other Bible texts such as: Psa. 106:37,38; Jer. 7:31; 19:5; Deut. 12:31; Ezekiel 16:20, 21; 23:37.

II Kings 17:16-17 is more explicit which is the culminating verse showing that the LORD was very unhappy with the Israelites in that period due to their practices which He demanded they not do including sacrificing their own children to pagan gods:

"They rejected all the commandments of the Lord their God and made for themselves cast images of two calves; they made a sacred pole, worshiped all the host of heaven, and served Baal. **They made their sons and their daughters pass through fire**; they used divination and augury; and they sold themselves to do evil in the sight of the Lord, provoking him to anger." (NRSV)

Notice in the text in II Kings 17:16 the use of the term "Baal". This term is a Hebrew word referring to false gods. It means "lord." There were several "Baals" (plural of Baal) referred to in the Bible. In the NRSV, this term appears 19 times in the Old Testament.

---

[80] Cyclopedia of Biblical, Theological and Ecclesiastical Literature (CBTEL), vol. VI, pg. 438

One of these "Baals" was "Baal of Peor". This phrase means "Lord of the opening" and is understood in an obscene sexual sense. One can review the following texts for more information about this deity (Numbers 25:1,3,5; Deut. 4:3; Psalm 106:28; Hosea 9:10). The LORD was not pleased at the worship practices of this deity which are mentioned in the previously mentioned texts. This is because this worship involved unnatural sexual practices which were unholy and condemned in the Old Testament.

What we see in these texts and in these practices is the pursuit of a lifestyle, practice and philosophy which see the perpetrators holding a total disregard for any sanctity of life to the point where one would murder their own offspring with unimaginable pain and suffering. People were offering their own children to pagan gods as burnt offerings! It is in this light that we must interpret the teaching of circumcision.

Concerning the Greco-Roman culture, we can refer to the research of Professor O. Bakke, whose book "*When Children Became People: The Birth of Childhood in Early Christianity*" is a helpful resource on this subject. What we find is in many ways much the same as our example from ANE culture.

Professor Bakke points out that within the Greco-Roman society itself, there existed a brutality which is hard to comprehend for us today, but was very much a part of that society at that time. A good example of this is what happened in the year 63 BCE and concerned a law issued in that year by the Roman Senate forbidding to raise boy babies in that year:

"According to Suetonius, one of Augustus's freedmen claimed that the Senate had issued a law in 63 B.C.E. because of an 'evil portent' forbidding parents to raise the boys born in that year." (Bakke, pg. 30)

This information is further mention by Ernest L. Martin referring to the same time showing how important astrological interpretations were in that period saying:

"This is especially so since astrological interpretations by official religious authorities were reckoned at the time to be of supreme value in interpreting historical events. There were probably as many or more people percentage-wise interested in astrology and astronomical occurrences at this period of history than any other in western civilization. Historical documents show how serious people were in regard to astrology. According to Julius Marathus, a personal confidant of Augustus Caesar, the Roman Senate in the year 63 B.C. ordered all to be killed who were born in that year because prophetic dreams and astrological signs suggested that a "King of the Romans" was to be born. The Senate ostensibly considered a "King of the Romans" to be anathema to the government of the Republic. Some senators, however, whose wives were pregnant refused to register births from their wives in hopes that the signs applied to them. We are informed that in that very year (23 September, 63 B.C.), the person who later became the first emperor of the Romans (Augustus) was born."[81]

This brutality against children in a wider societal sense is something that we also see illustrated in the horrifying behavior of King Herod, who murdered the innocent boys in Bethlehem under two years of age. (Matt. 2:16)

Bakke goes on to show that in Roman society, there were instances where some parents would kill (by *expositio*, exposing them to the elements causing their deaths) their children in protest to political, religious or social events taking place in the society at certain times:

---

[81] Martin, "The Star That Astonished the World", ASK Publication: Portland: OR, 1996, p.6.

"One specifically Roman phenomenon was the *expositio* of children as a kind of protest against the gods, in response to events that people felt were gravely unjust; Suetonius relates that when new spread of the death of Germanicus, the popular crown prince and father of Caligula, some parents reacted by exposing their children. If this did, in fact, occur, it may perhaps be interpreted 'as a societal suicide in response to a situation of anomy (social instability caused by erosion of standards or values).' In the rhetorical tradition, we find a view that the frequency of exposition was related to how the emperor ruled. 'It is a sign of a good emperor, in the universe of the rhetoricians, when parents want to raise up children; under a tyranny they expose them." (*ibid.*)

It is important to point out that while some children who were exposed to the elements may have been found by someone else and taken and raised, many of those exposed died:

"William W. Harris presents and discusses a broad spectrum of source materials that indicate that many of these exposed children did in fact die." (*ibid.* p. 32)

This issue of exposing children is an issue which was placed under the legal right of the father of the family.

"In a Roman family, the father (*paterfamilias*) has the legal right to decide the life or death of the other members of the family, and it was he, at least in the final instance, who decided whether a child should be accepted into the family or exposed." (*ibid.* p.29)

Rousseau and Arav also comment on the same matter saying:

"In Roman law children and slaves has the same status, both were property of the paterfamilias, both had the duty of obedience and service, and both could be sold."[82]

This societal custom of exposing children is contextualized into the Greco-Roman culture which also had views on newborn children that saw them as not quite human yet:

"The critical phase was the first eight to nine days, during which this question (whether the child would live and join the family or be exposed) was decided. The acceptance of the child as a family member was celebrated ritually in the home on the so-called *dies lustrios* ('day of purification') in the presence of the immediate family and relatives." (*ibid.*)

A number of issues were addressed in accepting the child into the family on this day:

"It was then that the child was given its name. This ceremony was held for boys on the eighth day after birth, for girls on the ninth day, and it marked the child's social birth, as opposed to its biological birth. The registry office was to be informed only after the child had received a name and been socially accepted into the family; this shows that social birth was more important or considered more fundamental than biological birth. In this period before its social birth, the child did not have the status of a juridical person as it did afterward. This seems to be because the child was not yet perceived as a full human being." (*ibid.*)

---

[82] Rousseau, John J. and Arav, Rami, Jesus & His World: An Archaeological and Cultural Dictionary. SCM Press Ltd: London, 1995. pg. 256.

Professor Bakke points out these collective events, but this brutality towards children was magnified down to the individual level affecting individual children. Bakke notes that poverty was main cause for exposition saying:

"As I have pointed out, poverty was the commonest cause for *expositio*." (*ibid.* p. 31)

In addition, Bakke notes that children who were physically deformed or bodily weak were often killed and not allowed to grow up:

"Finally, children with obvious physical deformities were usually prevented from growing up. Seneca the Younger indicates that in his day, such children were commonly drowned; sources from the early imperial period also mention drowning as a means of killing babies. However, it is more probably that the midwives examined the newborn children and eliminated those they thought unfit to live; it is also probable that some were exposed. According to Seneca, not only children with deformities were killed, but also those considered weak. The physician Soranus gives a long list of the criteria (some of them rather strict) a child must satisfy in order to be considered healthy enough to be allowed to grow up. We do not know to what extent his criteria were actually employed, but at any rate they show that is was societally acceptable to lay down criteria entailing that many babies would have been refused the right to grow up." (*ibid.*)

Of these reasons for not allowing children even to live, we must add to this preference for boys over girls. Speaking of exposing children, Bakke says the following:

"It is reasonable to assume that more girls than boys met with such a fate. Such a view is supported, though not definitively affirmed, in our sources, and many factors point in this direction. Since the firstborn boy was the (principal heir), it was important to 'ensure' that a couple had a son." (*ibid.*, pg. 31)

Some texts point to the idea of preferring a boy over a girl before a child is born:

"The words of an Egyptian man in the first century B.C.E. in a letter to his wife who was soon to bear a child, have become well known: 'If you chance to bear a child, and it is a boy, let it be; if it is a girl, expose it.'" (*ibid.*)

This general trend is not enough for us to confirm a wider societal trend, but here is where the science of archaeology helps to confirm these written statements.

"Obviously, this unparalleled utterance (talking about the above quote from Egypt), taken by itself, does not entitle us to draw far-reaching conclusions; a group of inscriptions from Delphi are more important in the search for representative texts. Scholars maintain that we can reconstruct six hundred families on the basis of this material, and only six of these families had more than one daughter. The simplest explanation of this disproportion seems to be that the parents got rid of female babies." (*ibid.*)

How Does This Situation in ANE/Roman Society Compare with Judaic Society?

Now that we have some data to help in our comparison, let us ask how the overall situation in the ANE/Greco-Roman world compared to the Jewish world?

To answer this question, it is useful to point out a general comment against exposing children made by Bakke concerning the opinion of a well-known Jewish scholar, who was also a recognized member of this Greco-Roman, Hellenized society.

"These observations on infanticide and *expositio* should not lead the reader to suppose that these practices received universal assent. The hellenized Jew Philo was the first to offer an explicit critique, affirming that it goes against the divine law." (*ibid.* pg. 32)

Philo was absolutely correct. Infanticide completely goes against everything we know about the Law of Moses and the value and desire that Hebraic culture placed on having children and bringing them up.

It is this environment that we have to consider when it comes to properly interpreting Proverbs 19:18, which is our focus text in this examination. Now that we can see the Greco-Roman context, how does this compare with the Hebraic, Biblical context and what Jewish believers in the Holy Scriptures believed and practiced? Once we see this, we can see Professor Webb's Redemptive Movement Hermeneutic (RMH) in clear operation because what we are going to find is that when we move from the ANE society to the Greco-Roman society into the Biblical Hebraic society of the Hebrew Bible followed by the Gospel message found in the New Testament, what we are going to find is a movement of ideas which are moving towards life, love, peace and gentleness away from death, indifference, brutality and violence.

The overall context which Philo mentioned of infanticide being against the divine law starts really in the very first chapters of Genesis with the first recognized commandment of the Law of Moses: Procreation (Genesis 1:28).

Jewish law saw in a child just born out the womb as a legally entitled individual. That child did not have to wait any time before it was legally considered a juridical person. A child becomes a "living being" when the breath of life enters the lungs. (Gen. 2:7) This always happens immediately after a child is first born as a necessity for survival.

The first commandment of the Law of Moses requires that one have children. This religious requirement has numerous other ideas attached to it that very greatly affect our interpretation of later Bible texts (like Proverbs). Notice some of the points that are attached to the idea of procreation, which were taught by later Jewish scholars:

- "When a man reaches the age of 18 he becomes subject to the *mitzvah* [the commandment] to marry and to have children." (Chill – footnote 96)
- "To fulfill the mitzvah adequately, a man must beget at least one son and one daughter who, in turn, must be physically capable of begetting children of their own. In other words, one has not fulfilled the mitzvah of procreation if, for example, he begets a son who is sexually impotent or a daughter who is barren."

When we consider these commentators views on procreation and having children, it is clear that within the law to procreate and have children, there is an understanding that the parents are going to care for the children from the first moments of their lives and to continue to do so for the future after that.

As for selecting who gets to live based on physical capacities, gender, social or economic standing, these issues have no relevance or standing before the law. All children are to be welcomed into the family and cared for equally as God's children. The Bible has stories of individuals who are adults who were born possessing physical challenges (see Acts 3:1-11), of families that have only girls (Numbers 27 & 36), of poor families and their members (Matthew 5:3). Regardless of any of these circumstances, just because one finds himself in facing one of these issues, there is never any kind of excuse to let a child die within Judaism.

Infanticide in the Law of Moses is murder and is a violation of sixth commandment. (Exodus 20:13) Coupled with this fact is the Jewish concept of *pikuach nefesh* (saving a life). This principle basically points out that in Jewish law that the preservation of life overrides virtually any other religious rule.[83] What we find is that this is almost the exact opposite of some of the cultural practices we have been discussing.

This understanding helps us better appreciate the Bible's teachings and the need to properly position them in the society where they originally conceived and to understand what those practices represented in those times and to properly orient them to the New Testament and the beliefs and realities put forward by our Lord Jesus and His disciples.

Conclusion

When we look at the disregard that ancient societies had for the lives of their children, we can now better understand how circumcision protected boy babies in particular from the horrors of human sacrifice.

These children were now sanctified through circumcision and made holy and as we have seen in this research study, oriented towards life, marriage and having their own families. A boy child could not be exposed or sacrificed because

---

[83] https://www.myjewishlearning.com/article/pikuach-nefesh-the-overriding-jewish-value-of-human-life/

94

he was destined to be dedicated to the LORD and physically marked as being in a covenant relationship with God. This provided immense protection to that child and required the parents to treat this baby boy with great care and love.

This was not the feeling of the ANE or Greco/Roman societies when it came to children. So, God introduced something which slowly began to move and alter the practices which the earth was dominated with before and during the time circumcision came into existence.

7. What were the intended societal impacts?

It is important now that we have understood circumcision's links to ethical sexual behavior in males and by extension to the whole of the community who are engaging in this ritual, we come to the important question of why it was done at such an early age.

The Bible commanded that all male children be circumcised on the eight day of life saying:

"This is my covenant, which you shall keep, between me and you and your offspring after you: Every male among you shall be circumcised. You shall circumcise the flesh of your foreskins, and it shall be a sign of the covenant between me and you. Throughout your generations every male among you shall be circumcised when he is eight days old, including the slave born in your house and the one bought with your money from any foreigner who is not of your offspring. Both the slave born in your house and the one bought with your money must be circumcised. So shall my covenant be in your flesh an everlasting covenant. Any uncircumcised male who is not circumcised in the flesh of his foreskin shall be cut off from his people; he has broken my covenant." (Genesis 17:10-14 NRSV)

Make no mistake about this teaching. Circumcision was an absolute requirement within the faith of Judaism. It is such an important teaching that its performance could be undertaken on the holiest day of the year, the Day of Atonement. (Chill, pg. 5) While this is the case, it also is a fact that if a child was not healthy enough to undertake the procedure, circumcision could be delayed until the child was in good enough health to undertake the procedure. (*ibid.*)

Now, some key points must be understood about circumcision by all of us so that we can really comprehend why it was done at such an early age.

First, we must understand that in the beginning stage of its having taken place on the body of an infant boy, only the family of the child and those in his immediate community would have been aware that this procedure had been undertaken upon the child. Dr. Martin has pointed this out in the earlier referenced paper.

This points to a very important teaching which we must understand. The child to whom the procedure happened had no knowledge of its significance when it was administered to him. However, what is very important to understand is what it signified to those in his immediate circle of life. The procedure made the child a "son of the covenant" of Abraham, but this covenant implied that this child was going to be raised in an environment where all aspects of that covenant were to be adhered to.

Within the Law of Moses, there have been enumerated 613 laws or commandments which were obligatory on men to keep (248 positive commandments) or to avoid (365 negative commandments) [Chill, xiv] Of course, some of these commandments applied only to men (certainly this one is an example of that – wearing *tzitzit* and a four cornered garment would be another one [Numbers 15:38])

It is also very important to understand the importance of circumcision in its close proximity in the Biblical text to another commandment that dealt very much with the most fundamental aspect of the Biblical covenantal society. What was this teaching? It is found in Genesis 1:28 saying:

"Be fruitful and multiply, and fill the earth, and subdue it."

Of course, you cannot have a covenantal society if that society is not perpetuated. This is why the commandment of procreation is so important and is given as the first commandment in all of the Holy Bible.

This first of the Biblical commandments is a most important one, which according to Rabbi Chill had some of the following requirements associated with it.

"When a man reaches the age of 18 he becomes subject to the mitzvah to marry and to have children.

The mitzvah (commandment in English) of procreation is incumbent only upon the male, not the female.

To fulfill this mitzvah adequately, a man must beget at least one son and one daughter, who, in turn, must be physically capable of begetting children of their own. …" (Chill, pg. 3)

It is no accident that the commandment of circumcision comes immediately after this first commandment of procreation found in Genesis 1:28. The reason for this is because in the early Biblical period prior to the cataclysmic destruction of the Earth by water (know commonly by the term "the Flood of Noah") and the subsequent recreation that took place in the time of Noah, the Bible records a number of events prior to the time when circumcision was introduced, which show the world participating in behaviors which the Bible later in the book of Leviticus 18 mentioned as being against God's design.

As has been discussed earlier in this volume, much of the information in the earlier chapters of Genesis is very terse and not much detail is given, but we do have in the first 17 chapters of Genesis quite a lot of information given which the teaching of circumcision comes at the very end of pointing a direction for mankind to pursue sexual purity.

This is important because circumcision was given 430 years before the Law of Moses was given. (Galatians 3:16,17) We have to look at other information to better understand the rationale and role of circumcision in this time before the Law of Moses had been given. This is because the administration under which Abraham received circumcision is different than that under which the Law of Moses was revealed.

We must first understand that the ethical rules and laws that governed the life and times Abraham lived were fundamentally different than later laws that were given through Moses. We have to first understand the meaning of circumcision in the time of Abraham and then supplement our understanding of this teaching through those given later by Moses. We must do this because there are some differences between what Abraham knew to be religious requirements that governed his life compared to those later teachings, which we must more extensive, given through Moses. An important quote in this regard which can really capture well this situation is the following:

"With the introduction of the covenant of circumcision between God and man (specifically with Abraham and his seed), religious requirements became more ritualistic and distinctive. But when Moses was commission-ed by God to give the Israelites His Old Covenant revelation, ceremonial-ism became even more pronounced. Indeed, the differences between the patriarchial religious system established in the time of Abraham and that begun in the time of Moses were as different as daylight and dark. Note the dissimilarities.

Under the Abrahamic covenant, God allowed His people to offer sacrifices anywhere they pleased (Gen. 12:7; 35:1: Job 1:5), but Moses changed this by commanding only the family of Aaron to attend to the sacred rites (Exo. 40:1-16), and those sacrifices could only be offered on the altar in the Sanctuary (Deut. 12:13,14). Abraham planted a grove (or sacred tree) in Beersheba (Gen. 21:33). But under Moses the use of groves became prohibited (11 Chron. 14:3: Isa. 17:8). Jacob set up a pilar Genesis 28: 18). but this was later forbidden by Moses Deut. (3:22, margin). God had said in the time of Noah: "Every moving thing i.e., all animals! that liveth shall be meat for you: even as the green herb have I given you all things" (Gen. 9:3), but with Moses, only the beasts which were mentioned in Leviticus 11 were allowed or disallowed. There were no official feast days commanded in the time of Abraham, but with Moses, the ordained festivals became commanded periods for attendance by all Israelite males (Lev. 23). Tithing was not a law in the patriarchial period (see our Tithing booklet), but with Moses, it became a strict dictate (Deut. 12:11). None of the Patriarchs wore phylacteries (at least we have no record of such), but with Moses. their use was commanded (Num. 15:37-41) The land did not have to rest every seventh year under the Patriarchs (Gen. 41:34,35), but with Moses, that too was changed (Lev. 25:1-7). Abraham even married his half-sister with God's approval (Genesis 20:12), but this became illegal in the time of Moses (Lev. 20:17), Abraham was also confederate with his Canaanite neighbors (Gen. 14:13), but no leagues with the Canaanites were allowed in the dispensation of Moses indeed, the Canaanites were to be exterminated (Deut. 20:17,18). There was also no commanded Sabbath law in the patriarchial period, but in the time of Moses the Sabbath was first introduced as a law (Neh. 9:14; Ezekiel 20:12) with many stringent requirements that changed the very character of the seventh day of the week. Moses had now come on the scene and what a profound change in religious essentials occurred.

The differences between the religious system of the Patriarchs and that of Moses were dramatic. Look at it this way. If a religious Israelite in the time of David (well within the Mosaic dispensation) could have been transported back to Abraham's time and witnessed Abraham (not knowing who he was) performing his religious duties, he would no doubt have called him an unconverted heathen. For the first ninety-nine years of Abraham's life, he wasn't circumcised: then later he built altars anywhere he pleased; he raised up groves; he offered no lamb at Passover; he kept no weekly Sabbath; he attended no holy feasts; he wore no phylacteries; he married his half-sister; kept no land sabbath; and of all things, he was allied with the Canaanites.

Actually. what God did in Moses' time was to rescind the religious requirements of the patriarchial period in favor of the more strict laws ordained in the time of Moses. The two religious systems were so completely different from one another that were one to try mixing them together utter confusion would result.

However, there are some people who are so conservative that they will not allow God to bring in new religious systems different from previous ones. They cannot believe that God changes His mind (and He doesn't in overall philosophical matters). But God has most decidedly changed whole religious systems in the past, and these alterations are recorded in the Bible."[84]

Circumcision radically redirected Abraham and his descendants in the direction of holiness, which was going to be reinforced with further instructions given by the LORD in the Law of Moses given 430 years after the Abrahamic covenant.

---

[84] Martin, E. "Progressive Revelation", Foundation for Biblical Research, Pasadena: CA, 1975.

8.   Circumcision: Its Link to Baptism it in the Early Church

Earlier in this manuscript, I have noted that most Christians are generally clear about the biblical teachings surrounding circumcision for the Christian and that for non-Jewish believers. There is a precise teaching in the New Testament showing that circumcision is not mandatory.[85] While for most Christians, this issue is fairly clear from a religious practice point of view, what is lesser known or understood are the links that early Christian scholars found between the teaching of circumcision and infant baptism. For many early Christian scholars, infant baptism became like a spiritual circumcision, one made without hands and not directly in the fleshly body. They found in infant baptism a way to connect baptism to circumcision by saying that baptized infants became a part of the New Covenant and were thereby saved in Christ through infant baptism much in the same way that infant boys joined of the Abrahamic covenant through being circumcised.

As we have shown herein, circumcision was linked to a personal consecration to God on behalf of the individual which was recognized by the community in which that boy child lived and was to grow up. It signified that this child was going to be different than other people, he would be holy, sanctified and set apart and raised by his parents and his community to be consecrated to God in his life, behavior and especially in his orientation to sexual purity, procreation, marriage, having children and living a holy, sanctified life. Circumcision also provided a protection to the infant boy to dedicate him to the LORD and protect his life in a way not previously provided in the time before the practice was initiated by the LORD.

---

[85] Acts 15; Galatians 5:2

As Christians, we note the similarities of the above noted points found solidly anchored in baptism. Note the important statements in this regard in CBTEL saying:

"The ethical and spiritual value of circumcision did not depend on its existence or use prior to its adoption by God as a symbol of true religion. The condescension of Christ consecrated and elevated old rites to new spheres, if the principle that 'what God hath cleansed, that call not thou common.' (Acts 10:15; 11:9) On this principle he elected the baptismal purification, and the simple elements of his Supper." (CBTEL, Vol. II, pg. 352)

In regard to Christian baptism, we can understand the rationale for it in the life of the Christian believer as follows:

"It (baptism) must be preceded by faith (Acts 8:13; 10:33) and repentance (Acts 2:38), and acc. to St. Paul effects and represents the believer's union with Christ through which he participates in His death and resurrection (Romans 6:4), is cleansed from his sins (I Corinthians 6:11), and incorporated into the Body of Christ. (I Corinthians 12:13)" (Cross, The Oxford Dictionary of the Christian Church, pg. 120)

Here it is very important to quote also Colossians 2:8-14, which provides a very close link between circumcision and baptism. Note it here saying:

"See to it that no one takes you captive by philosophy and empty deceit, according to human tradition, according to the elemental spirits of the world, and not according to Christ. For in him the whole fullness of deity dwells bodily, and you have been filled in him, who is the head of all rule and authority. In him also you were circumcised **with a circumcision made without hands,** by putting off the body of the flesh, by the circumcision of Christ, **having been buried with him in baptism,** in which you were also raised with him through faith in the powerful working of God, who raised him from the dead. And you, who were dead in your trespasses and the uncircumcision of your flesh, God made alive together with him, having forgiven us all our trespasses, by canceling the record of debt that stood against us with its legal demands. This he set aside, nailing it to the cross." (ESV)

This text really makes the link clear. Note the following explanatory note from CBTEL saying:

"The writers of the New Testament bear testimony to the view here presented. St. Paul uses the very impressive words "buried with him" (Christ) "in baptism" – (Colossians 2:12), as synonymous with and explanatory of "the circumcision of Christ." Whatever intensity there is in the words "buried with him," it was only the effort of the apostle to show how "baptism into Christ" was like circumcision; it **"put off the body of the sins of the flesh."** Had such not been the scriptural meaning of circumcision, Paul would never have thus reasoned. What better testimony could be desired to prove the relation of the two rites and that the one had succeeded the other?" (*ibid.* pg. 353)

As we will see circumcision does have a future role in God's plan, but in this dispensation for Christians, there is definitely in this text a link between circumcision and baptism.

This view is not an isolated one, but is in fact well attested to among ancient Christian authorities:

"The early ecclesiastical writers universally held the views here given (in the quotes above). Their doctrine, made dependent on John 3:5, that baptism of water and the Spirit, was equivalent to regeneration by water and the Spirit, caused them to speak of baptism as spiritual circumcision, because the Spirit was always joined with the water in the baptism of an infant, or a converted, believing adult." (*ibid.*)

Numerous testimonies of this view are presented as follows saying:

"In Justin Martyr (who lived in the early 2nd century) baptism is very frequently alluded to as the "true circumcision," of which the ancient rite was a type (Apol. I,61; Dial. c. Trypho, 41) 'God commands you to be washed with this purification, and to be circumcised with the true circumcision' (Dial. c. Trypho Paragraph 18) He says that Christians 'had not received the fleshly circumcision, but the spiritual one, which Enoch and those like him made us of; and we received it through baptism." etc. (ibid Paragraph 43); comp. Paragraph 19) (*ibid.*)

Justin Martyr adds another relevant testimony saying:

"In paragraph 29 of this dialogue (with Trypho) he speaks of circumcision under the law as baptism. He says: 'What need have I for circumcision who have the testimony of God in my favor? ... What need have I of that other baptism, who have been baptized with the Holy Ghost?'" (*ibid.*)

CBTEL comments on this statement by Justin as follows:
"This must be esteemed as a remarkable identification of the two rites, for we should not forget that, as the ordination of baptism was to Justin 'the water of

life' (Dial. C. Trypho Paragraph 14), so to receive it was to be baptized with the Holy Ghost." (*ibid.*)

Justin Martyr also said the following:

"We are circumcised by baptism, by Christ's circumcision." ((*ibid.* vol. I, pg. 648)

We also have the following note about baptism and circumcision from St. Basil:

"From the same point of view (as Justin Martyr), Basil asks certain one who delayed baptism 'Do you put off the *circumcision made without hands* – in putting off the flesh, *which is performed in baptism?*" (*ibid.*)

We also have an important reference from Tertullian saying:

"On the principle that Christ was the real baptized in the Christian rite, Tertullian calls Christ, 'the Purifier of the new circumcision.'" (*ibid.*)

We can see in these references from very early Christian authorities that they believed that there was a link between the baptism of infants and circumcision. They believed that both of them had links to holy behavior and a recognition of the need to reduce the influence of the flesh in the lives of those taking part in those rituals.

9. Circumcision: Understanding why early Jewish Christians advocated for the Circumcision of Gentiles

Now that we can understand that circumcision is very closely linked to ethical behavior in the area of the sexual life specifically of men, some of the texts in the New Testament can begin to make more sense. When we make this connection, the whole understanding of circumcision in the New Testament starts to become much clearer especially when we consider the environment of the early Christian Church community which originated in Jerusalem after the year 30AD and the death of Jesus.

Christians have a tendency to think that circumcision for us has been made irrelevant in light of the death of Jesus Christ (Acts 15: Galatians 5:2) and is a practice which we need no longer to pay any attention to. While this is indeed true, we must realize that circumcision is not something that has been forever forgotten or will no longer have any role in the plan of God for humanity.

For many Christians, such a statement may seem, on the surface, almost nonsensical and even impossible in light of seemingly "clear" teachings given in particular by St. Paul in the books of Romans and Colossians. Herein lies an opportunity for learning and for a greater understanding of God's plan for mankind if we are just willing to put aside mistaken assumptions based upon an incomplete understanding of what is going to take place on this earth when Jesus returns at the Second Coming.

We are not here talking about some wild, mystical idea. In no way! Why? Because what we are going to be discussing is an understanding that existed in the earliest Christian community that was based in Jerusalem and who had an accurate understanding of what was going to happen immediately after Jesus returned. In their mind, the teaching of circumcision and its applicability in their minds based upon what they knew was soon to take place on earth. For these early believers, it was completely logical that circumcision would have a role in society and that role extended to all who were in communion with Jesus Christ and His message and kingdom. Let us see how this is the case.

The role of Circumcision in God's Economy after Christ's Second Coming

After the death of Jesus Christ, we are informed in the book of Acts that immediately upon His being raised from the dead and being on earth for 40 days after which the day of Pentecost came and the Holy Spirit arrived and began the ministry of the Spirit in the early Church, what is clear is that all, and I mean all, of the first earliest believers in Jesus were also believing adherents to Judaism. (Acts 2:5, 14, 22) However, this was not to continue. This is because the message of the Gospel began to be heard and accepted by Gentile believers as well as those first Jewish believers. (Acts 8:26-39; Acts 10) These are basic facts about the beginnings of Christianity in which all Christians agree. But it was not too long before some concerns were brought forward to the early Church that had to be addressed and one of these involved the issue of circumcision.

It is important that we realize that this issue has a context, has a relevance and must be understood to be based on the future reality that early Jews expected would be in evidence in the Messianic Age. These teachings were not mystical or based on allegories or parables. They were practically understood to come into force because this is the exact teaching found in the prophets of God whose writings in the Hebrew Bible are inspired Scripture.

Many believers stop thinking about circumcision after the controversy in Acts 15 thinking the whole matter was solved at that time and that no further discussion of this matter is merited. This view must be rethought.

Now as the ministry of the Church began to reach out to Gentile believers through the ministry of St. Peter and then St. Paul and Barnabas prior to Acts 15, a new question arose put forth by Jewish believers in Jesus Christ concerning the need for non-Jewish believers to be circumcised and keep the Law of Moses, or else they would not be saved. Note the exact statement concerning this from Acts 15:1:

"But some men came down from Judea and were teaching the brothers, "**Unless you are circumcised** according to the custom of Moses, you cannot be saved." (Acts 15:1 ESV)

Now, this became a very serious matter, which needed to be addressed because those who were putting this idea forward were not doing so with no rationale, specific reasoning or Biblical authority. On the contrary, they had a very strong Scriptural basis for making this suggestion. Let us consider this evidence because it is very important to our discussion here at hand about the question of circumcision.

Now, let us first understand a very clear point, which we must understand concerning the actions of these Jewish brethren and what was motivating them to make this suggestion that even to Gentile believers in Jesus Christ had to be circumcised and keep the Law of Moses. This point is the understanding that these believers (like most of the Christians in the early formative period of the early church from 30AD – 63 AD) believed that Jesus was almost certainly going to be returning from heaven and would be establishing the heavenly kingdom that was promised to all believers in the Bible in their lifetimes. That is correct. Bible believers at that time believed strongly that Jesus was very soon to return from heaven almost certainly in their own lifetimes and this idea was what was motivating most people (even including the Apostles) in the early period of the formation of the Christian Church. Let us see the evidence for this idea.

Note also the following Biblical texts from the New Testament which make it clear that even the Apostles up until just before the year 70 AD believed that they were living in the last generation on earth before Jesus Christ would return from heaven and set up His heavenly kingdom on this earth. Note first Matthew 16:28, which says:

"Truly, I say to you, there are some standing here who will not taste death until they see the Son of Man coming in his kingdom."

Of course, the apostles had this explicit statement of Christ, which was heard by the disciples and was believed by them.

Even at the time Christ returned to heaven, He told them when they asked about His return, He said:

"So when they had come together, they asked him, "Lord, is this the time when you will restore the kingdom to Israel?" He replied, "It is not for you to know the times or periods that the Father has set by his own authority." (Acts 1:6,7 NRSV)

This statement was not 100% clear to the apostles who, in the early period discussed in the book of Acts, point strongly to the idea that Christ would be returning soon.

The book of Acts shows the belief in soon coming return of Jesus. The arrival of the Holy Spirit on the Day of Pentecost shows how Peter in particular interpreted what was happening at that time. What was happening to his mind showed that the end of that current age was soon to arrive and a new millennial age was to start with the return of Jesus.

"But Peter, standing with the eleven, raised his voice and addressed them, "Men of Judea and all who live in Jerusalem, let this be known to you, and listen to what I say. Indeed, these are not drunk, as you suppose, for it is only nine o'clock in the morning. No, this is what was spoken through the prophet Joel:

'In the last days it will be, God declares,
that I will pour out my Spirit upon all flesh,
   and your sons and your daughters shall prophesy,
and your young men shall see visions,
   and your old men shall dream dreams.
Even upon my slaves, both men and women,
   in those days I will pour out my Spirit;
     and they shall prophesy.
And I will show portents in the heaven above
   and signs on the earth below,
     blood, and fire, and smoky mist.
The sun shall be turned to darkness
   and the moon to blood,
     before the coming of the Lord's great and glorious day.
Then everyone who calls on the name of the Lord shall be saved.'"
(Acts 2:14-22 NRSV)

As clear as Peter could make it, he believed at that time that the end of the age was soon to take place. This idea continues in Acts 3:19-21, where Peter again urged the hearers of his sermon to repent and see the return of Jesus take place saying:

"Repent therefore, and turn to God so that your sins may be wiped out, so that times of refreshing may come from the presence of the Lord, and that he may send the Messiah appointed for you, that is, Jesus, who must remain in heaven until the time of universal restoration that God announced long ago through his holy prophets." (Acts 3:19-21 NRSV)

The late New Testament scholar, Prof. F.F. Bruce, comments on his view concerning the beliefs being expressed in these early sections of Acts which are also reflect in some of Paul's later ideas saying the following:

"The early currency of the invocation *maranatha* bears witness to the disciples' lively expectation of Jesus' parousia, his advent in glory, to consumate the kingdom inaugurated by his death and resurrection. One of the most primitive eschatological passages in the New Testament come in Peter's exhortation to the people of Jerusalem to repent and turn gain, so that their sins may be blotted out and "that time of refreshing may come from the presence of the Lord", with the sending of Jesus, their foreordained Messiah, "whom heaven must receive until the time for establishing all that God spoke by the mouth of his holy prophets from of old" (Acts 3;19-21). Here it is implied that early expectation was soon superseded by others, but the expectation itself lived on as a potent hope throughout the apostolic age, not least in the thought of Paul."[86]

---

[86] Bruce, F.F. Paul: Apostle of the Heart Set Free, Grand Rapids, MI: Eerdmans:1977, 67.

Note importantly in Acts 4:34-5:11 we have the teachings concerning several early Christians who sold their properties and gave all the money to the early Church. It is clear that such an approach would have been undertaken by people who loved God deeply and were thankful for His work and mercy, but also on a practical level, those same people were giving up their own personal livelihoods, so it is reasonable that these people thought they were living in a miraculous existence and this had an influence on their decisions to give away their physical assets linked to their own livelihoods.

Note also the very clear statement of St. Paul where he said in First Corinthians that the "time was short".

"This is what I mean, brothers: **the appointed time has grown very short**. From now on, let those who have wives live as though they had none, and those who mourn as though they were not mourning, and those who rejoice as though they were not rejoicing, and those who buy as though they had no goods, and those who deal with the world as though they had no dealings with it. **For the present form of this world is passing away.** (1 Corinthians 7:29-31 ESV)

Paul, of course, was echoing the words of our Lord who said this in Matt. 24:19:

"And alas for women who are pregnant and for those who are nursing infants in those days!" (Matthew 24:19 ESV)

It may seem strange to us, but this is the precise teaching of St. Paul who later had a more accurate understanding than this earlier teaching when writing to Timothy saying:

113

"So I would have younger widows marry, bear children, manage their households, and give the adversary no occasion for slander." (1 Timothy 5:14 ESV)

There are other factors which made the early apostles think that Jesus was returning in their lifetimes, however, the issue raised in Acts 15:1 of the need for Gentiles to keep the Law of Moses and become physically circumcised has to be understood as coming from an orientation which believed that in one form the kingdom of God had already arrived in some sense or that it was very soon to arrive. Why is this? Let us look at this question now.

The Age to Come and the place of the Gentile believer in that system

It was the express teaching of Jesus Christ when He returned to heaven on the 40th day after His resurrection that it was His intention to return to earth. At some time in the future (and as He left bodily and rose up to heaven from the Mount of Olives), He told us (and it is recorded in the book of Acts) that He would return back to earth from heaven and that His feet would one day in the future touch again from the exact spot He left earth on that 40th day. This is the exact teaching of Acts 1:

"And when he had said these things, as they were looking on, he was lifted up, and a cloud took him out of their sight. And while they were gazing into heaven as he went, behold, two men stood by them in white robes, and said, "Men of Galilee, why do you stand looking into heaven? This Jesus, who was taken up from you into heaven, will come in the same way as you saw him go into heaven." (Acts 1:9-11 ESV)

So, it became the teaching of the Church that Jesus Christ would return to the Mount of Olives in the future. In fact, this idea is well known in the Old Testament where in Zechariah 14 it says:

"Then the LORD will go out and fight against those nations as when he fights on a day of battle. On that day his feet shall stand on the Mount of Olives that lies before Jerusalem on the east, and the Mount of Olives shall be split in two from east to west by a very wide valley, so that one half of the Mount shall move northward, and the other half southward." (Zechariah 14:3-4 ESV)

These texts really speak about the same event and we have another text which elaborates further what will be taking place when Jesus returns concerning other matters in addition to His physical presence. Note what II Thessalonians 1:7,8 says:

"and to grant relief to you who are afflicted as well as to us, when the Lord Jesus is revealed from heaven with his mighty angels in flaming fire, ..." (2 Thessalonians 1:7-8 ESV)

Now this idea is linked to the first two texts we have referenced here about the return of the Lord Jesus Christ from heaven, but St. Paul here is quoting directly from the Old Testament and here is where we start to understand better the orientation of those dear brethren who were urging Gentile believers to keep the Law of Moses and become circumcised. Note the reference Paul is here quoting because it is very instructive for all of us to help us better understand the future in fact as well as the past. This next text is such an important one as it helps us put a lot of flesh on the overall skeleton of what it was that Jewish believers had in their minds about what the future entailed for not only themselves but also Gentile believers.

"For behold, the LORD will come in fire, and his chariots like the whirlwind, to render his anger in fury, and his rebuke with flames of fire. For by fire will the LORD enter into judgment, and by his sword, with all flesh; and those slain by the LORD shall be many. … And from them I will send survivors to the nations, to Tarshish, Pul, and Lud, who draw the bow, to Tubal and Javan, to the coastlands far away, that have not heard my fame or seen my glory. And they shall declare my glory among the nations. And they shall bring all your brothers from all the nations as an offering to the LORD, on horses and in chariots and in litters and on mules and on dromedaries, to my holy mountain Jerusalem, says the LORD, just as the Israelites bring their grain offering in a clean vessel to the house of the LORD. And some of them also I will take for priests and for Levites, says the LORD. For as the new heavens and the new earth that I make shall remain before me, says the LORD, so shall your offspring and your name remain. From new moon to new moon, and from Sabbath to Sabbath, all flesh shall come to worship before me, declares the LORD." (Isaiah 66:15-23 ESV)

This text starts to help us better understand why it was that in Acts 15:1 the early first Jewish believers in Christ in Jerusalem proposed to ask non-Jewish believers in Jesus to keep the Law of Moses and become circumcised. The text shows in the context after the second coming of Christ mentioned in the first verse that there is going to be a holy mountain in Jerusalem to which people from all over the world are going to come. Note that there will be priests and Levites, who are the ceremonial workers associated with a Temple, which will be in existence at that time. Five nations are mentioned as are "all flesh" as well as time periods such as the Sabbath and new moons.

What we have here is a picture which the Jewish believers in Jesus, who thought they were living in or fast approaching the Messianic age would have been very familiar with. So, it is much easier for us to see why they would suggest that Gentile start keeping the Law of Moses and to become circumcised. This is only the beginning of this explanation because we did not yet reach the discussion of circumcision specifically. But let's add more flesh onto this skeleton. Note another text which we quoted earlier which speaks about this same period:

"Then the LORD will go out and fight against those nations as when he fights on a day of battle. On that day his feet shall stand on the Mount of Olives that lies before Jerusalem on the east, and the Mount of Olives shall be split in two from east to west by a very wide valley, so that one half of the Mount shall move northward, and the other half southward. And you shall flee to the valley of my mountains, for the valley of the mountains shall reach to Azal. And you shall flee as you fled from the earthquake in the days of Uzziah king of Judah. Then the LORD my God will come, and all the holy ones with him. (Zechariah 14:3-5 ESV)

This text is very similar to Isaiah 66 and II Thessalonians 1, but it does add some additional information. It talks about some of the seismic disturbances to take place in the Jerusalem area when the LORD appears from heaven.

Note though in the same chapter what also is mentioned.

"On that day there shall be no light, cold, or frost. And there shall be a unique day, which is known to the LORD, neither day nor night, but at evening time there shall be light. On that day living waters shall flow out from Jerusalem, half

117

of them to the eastern sea and half of them to the western sea. It shall continue in summer as in winter. And the LORD will be king over all the earth. On that day the LORD will be one and his name one. **The whole land shall be turned into a plain from Geba to Rimmon south of Jerusalem.**[87] But Jerusalem shall remain aloft on its site from the Gate of Benjamin to the place of the former gate, to the Corner Gate, and from the Tower of Hananel to the king's winepresses. And it shall be inhabited, for there shall never again be a decree of utter destruction. Jerusalem shall dwell in security. (Zechariah 14:6-11 ESV)

This text elaborates with more information about that coming period in the future. The first verse talks about an astronomical phenomenon which is linked to the appearance of the harvest moon, where during that autumn period, you can almost read a book from the light that comes from the moon, so the daylight period almost exists for 24 hours.

It also speaks about the major seismic disturbances to take place in the Jerusalem area with the whole area being raised up and made a level plain. This level plain will be about sixty miles from north to south and on the top of that plain will be Jerusalem and from that city a spring of water will issue forth and water the Mediterranean Sea and the Dead Sea.

This matter is discussed and referenced by the late Dr. E. W. Bullinger in the Companion Bible, Appendix 88, has the following illustration which shows this square platform, which is a plain on top of an elevated area:

---

[87] See the figure on the next page which illustrates this written description exactly.

THE PORTION OF THE
"OBLATION"
FOR THE LEVITES

25,000 x 10,000 REEDS
= c. 60 MILES BY 24 = AN
AREA OF 1440 SQ. MILES

THE PORTION OF THE "OBLATION"
FOR THE PRIESTS

THE

SANCTUARY

25,000 x 10,000 REEDS
= 60 MILES BY 24 = AN
AREA OF 1440 SQ. MILES

THE PRINCE'S PORTION W.

THE CITY

THE PRINCE'S PORTION E.

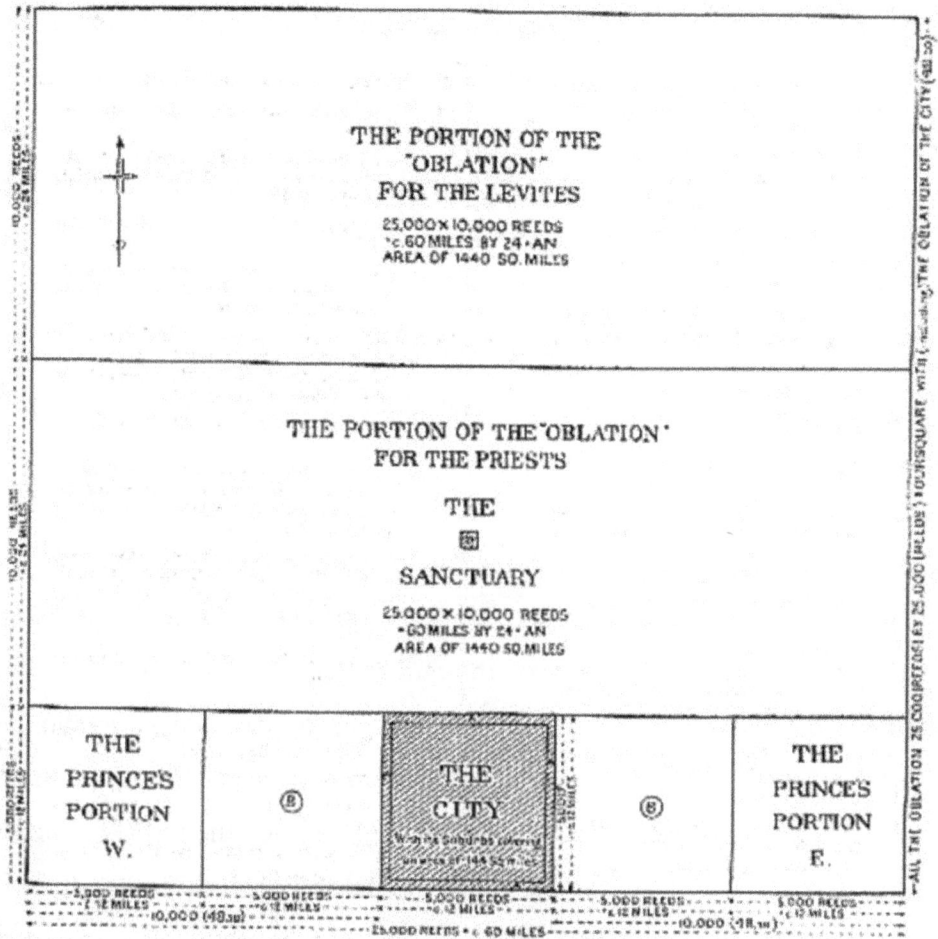

THE "POSSESSION OF THE CITY" LIES PARALLEL WITH THE "VERY GREAT VALLEY" of Zech. 14, 4, 5; which valley probably will form the Southern boundary of the City (see note on p. 126, par. 9).

Dr. Bullinger says the following in that same Appendix 88 from the Companion Bible:

"That "the Possession of the City" will lie parallel with "the great valley" cloven through the Mount of Olives and running east and west (Zech. 14:4, 5) seems clear. The "City of the Great King" will therefore be situated in a magnificent position on the north side of this great valley. No wonder it is spoken of as "beautiful for situation" (elevation, or extension). As the original Zion towered

119

above the Kidron Valley in days gone by, so in the Messianic days to come, "Zion, the City of our God" will be seen towering in majestic elevation above the north side of the "very great valley" that will then "cleft" east and west, and through which the cleansing waters will flow eastward to make the land, now desert, "blossom as the rose" (47:8 : and cp. Isa. 35).[88]

This is where the material starts to get very interesting in our current discussion. Before we get into that though, there is one other text in this same chapter which needs reference.

"Then everyone who survives of all the nations that have come against Jerusalem shall go up year after year to worship the King, the LORD of hosts, and to keep the Feast of Booths. And if any of the families of the earth do not go up to Jerusalem to worship the King, the LORD of hosts, there will be no rain on them. And if the family of Egypt does not go up and present themselves, then on them there shall be no rain; there shall be the plague with which the LORD afflicts the nations that do not go up to keep the Feast of Booths. This shall be the punishment to Egypt and the punishment to all the nations that do not go up to keep the Feast of Booths." (Zechariah 14:16-19 ESV)

This is a super important text because it reiterates what Isaiah 66 says in the sense that **the festival periods of the Law of Moses are going to be reinstituted** when Jesus Christ returns to earth at His Second Coming. Notice here that this text is not only directed at the nation and people of Israel! That is correct. All of the nations and all peoples are going to be required to keep this feast of Booths

---

[88] Dr. E. W. Bullinger, The Companion Bible, The Lamp Press, Ltd. London: England, Appendix 88, Pgs. 125-128.

(or the Feast of Tabernacles as many of us are familiar with it) after Jesus Christ returns.

Now, if the early Jewish believers mentioned in Acts 15:1 were urging the non-Jewish Christians to keep the Law of Moses and even become circumcised, we can start to understand why.

Now, let us look at several other texts from the book of Ezekiel which make this clearer and are speaking about the same period. We note that in Zechariah 14:8, it says:

"On that day living waters shall flow out from Jerusalem, half of them to the eastern sea and half of them to the western sea. It shall continue in summer as in winter." (Zechariah 14:8 ESV)

Now compare this text in Zechariah to the following text from the prophet Ezekiel, who said:

"Then he brought me back to the door of the temple, and behold, water was issuing from below the threshold of the temple toward the east (for the temple faced east). The water was flowing down from below the south end of the threshold of the temple, south of the altar. Then he brought me out by way of the north gate and led me around on the outside to the outer gate that faces toward the east; and behold, the water was trickling out on the south side. Going on eastward with a measuring line in his hand, the man measured a thousand cubits, and then led me through the water, and it was ankle-deep. Again he measured a thousand, and led me through the water, and it was knee-deep. Again he measured a thousand, and led me through the water, and it was waist-deep. Again he measured a thousand, and it was a river that I could not pass through, for the water had risen. It was deep enough to swim in, a river that could not be passed through. And he said to me, "Son of man, have you seen this?" Then he led me back to the bank of the river. As I went back, I saw on the bank of the river very many trees on the one side and on the other. And he said to me, "This water flows toward the eastern region and goes down into the Arabah, and enters the sea; when the water flows into the sea, the water will become fresh. And wherever the river goes, every living creature that swarms will live, and there will be very many fish. For this water goes there, that the waters of the sea may become fresh; so everything will live where the river goes. Fishermen will stand beside the sea. From Engedi to Eneglaim it will be a place for the spreading of nets. Its fish will be of very many kinds, like the fish of the Great Sea. But its swamps and marshes will not become fresh; they are to be left for salt. And on the banks, on both sides of the river, there will grow all kinds of trees for food. Their leaves will not wither, nor their fruit fail, but they will bear fresh fruit every month, because the water for them flows from the sanctuary. Their fruit will be for food, and their leaves for healing." (Ezekiel 47:1-12 ESV)

These two texts are really speaking about the same event, but in Ezekiel we have a little more elaboration. But that is not all that Ezekiel has to say and here is where it gets very interesting and relevant concerning the issue of circumcision. Note it here because all of Ezekiel from chapters 40-48 are speaking about the Messianic Age to come when Jesus Christ will be here on this earth:

"Thus says the Lord GOD: No foreigner, **uncircumcised in heart and flesh,** of all the foreigners who are among the people of Israel, shall enter my sanctuary." (Ezekiel 44:9 ESV)

This text on the surface doesn't seem to make rational sense based on many of the ideas many of us have inherited from our religious upbringing, but make no mistake about it, this very simple teaching shows that in the Age to Come, the Millennial reign of Jesus Christ for 1,000 years on this earth after He returns from heaven, the Law of Moses is going to be reinstituted and a key part of the keeping of that law for males **will involve them being circumcised**. Now why is the religious ritual of circumcision going to be reinstituted in the Millennial Age? To understand the answer to this question, we need to consider three very important issues, which are:

1. The New Covenant
2. The Resurrections of the Dead in the Millennial Age to Come
3. The Sabbath and its Spiritual Meaning

**To understand God's whole counsel,
we also need to understand the end of this teaching**

Circumcision is a part of the Mosaic covenant, called by the Christians the Old Covenant. The Old Covenant is made up of 613 commandments which were required to be kept by God by the ancient (and modern) Israelites. Circumcision is the second commandment found in the Old Testament. To me (and I am sure that I am not alone), on the surface, the whole idea seems to be somewhat strange and extreme. On the surface, when you read the accounts in the Bible where this practice is mentioned, it all just seems a bit strange and very difficult to understand it in a sensible way. It just does not seem to make any rationale sense on the surface. But here is where we really need to look at the whole counsel of God to find out what this subject really means.

Circumcision is a part of the system of the Mosaic Law, which in the New Testament is known as the first covenant. (Hebrews 8:7) That same book of Hebrews speaks about a second covenant, which the Old Testament refers to as "the New Covenant" and it refers to the passage from the book of Jeremiah where it is mentioned saying:

"For if that first covenant had been faultless, there would have been no occasion to look for a second. For he finds fault with them when he says: "Behold, the days are coming, declares the Lord, when I will establish a new covenant with the house of Israel and with the house of Judah, not like the covenant that I made with their fathers on the day when I took them by the hand to bring them out of the land of Egypt. For they did not continue in my covenant, and so I showed no concern for them, declares the Lord. For this is the covenant that I will make with the house of Israel after those days, declares the Lord: *I will put my laws into their minds, and write them on their hearts, and I will be their God, and they shall be my people. And they shall not teach, each one his neighbor and each one his brother, saying, 'Know the Lord,' for they shall all know me, from the least of them to the greatest. For I will be merciful toward their iniquities, and I will remember their sins no more.*" (Heb. 8:7-12 ESV)

Now, it is clear to most people I think that we have not entered into this "New Covenant" circumstance yet, but one day in the future, this will happen according to God's Word.

When we review the above referenced bold and italicized texts concerning the New Covenant, it is fundamentally different than the Old Covenant. External physical ceremonies will be done away with (including circumcision). It is a fundamentally new orientation and relationship between God and humanity.

However, prior to that time when the New Covenant will be introduced, we have a number of Scriptural texts in the Bible which show that after Jesus Christ returns to earth at His Second Coming, the First Covenant (or the Old Covenant, which included circumcision) is going to be reintroduced to the human beings that are living on earth at that time.

10. Circumcision and Intuition:

When your gut feeling tells you "No!" and You Know the Truth

One of the facts that a researcher encounters in the Christian context when it comes to the subject of circumcision is an aversion to the practice on the part of Christian mothers who just know deep down in their hearts and souls that circumcision is wrong for them. I can state categorically that there is a deep similarity between how Christian mothers in particular feel about the subjects of circumcision and spanking/smacking/corporal punishment. I have heard scores of times from numerous Christian women that they know that both practices go against their own personal gut feelings and maternal intuitions.

Unfortunately, today, Christian mothers often do not receive needed support to foster, honor and agree with these maternal intuitions.[89] In fact, in many cases, just the opposite occurs. Christian mothers are told to ignore these gut feelings or intuitions and just get their children circumcised.

What happens very often is that Christian mothers who give in to these pressures and go ahead and circumcise their sons develop a guilt that never goes away. You see this guilt manifested in how Christian women talk about themselves relative to the subject of circumcision. They often refer to themselves as "regret mothers." A whole language has developed around this concept.

For many mothers, this regret never ever goes away. This is often because they knew when they did it that their decision was wrong for them, but didn't have the support they needed (for many reasons) to hold their ground and not go through with the procedure on their sons.

---

[89] For a very detailed discussion on the whole subject of maternal intuition in the Bible, see my work "Thy Rod and Thy Staff, They Comfort Me: Book III – A Biblical Study on Maternal Intuition and its link to the Issue of Spanking Children" Amazon for hard copy & e-book formats. https://www.amazon.com/Samuel-artin/e/B00HP94ZZA/ref=dp_byline_cont_pop_book_1

In the Christian context, Christian women need Biblical evidence to Support their Choices concerning the subject of Gut Feelings or Intuition

When it comes to the subject of gut feelings or intuition, these subjects for many Christians are considered off limits. Christian women are told to ignore and turn off these feelings being told to listen to their husbands, male relatives or pastors. These feelings are very much linked closely to the subject matter we are talking about relative to intuition because these "gut feelings" for Christian mothers who have communicated with me are very, very real.

These "gut feelings" are one way that has been described to me that intuitive truths are communicated to women. Their reality is just as real and practical as their acquired knowledge which is passed on through verbal or literate means. [While both sexes may have "gut feelings", we are focused here on women's and mother's experience with this phenomenon.] Having said this, the support mechanisms available for Christian women in cultivating and listening to and honoring these gut feelings is still today very limited and in many cases non-existent. Thankfully, today many women are speaking out and sharing their experiences, but what is also needed is a solid Biblical teaching concerning this subject of gut feelings or intuition. This is because if there is a natural reality of "gut feelings" or in particular "maternal intuition" which is attested by numerous Christian mothers (who have communicated with me), it seems logical that we should find some more specific allusions to this matter in the Bible? I think that most reasonable people would think that God, who is all knowing, may have given us some practical and specific teaching about this subject. While the information on this subject may not be exactly pinpointed in Scripture in modern terms, if we have eyes to see and ears to hear and we are open to God's Word, we may find more on this subject in Scripture than we previously may have thought or realized.

Hearing Christian Mother's Voices:
A First Step to Understand "Gut Feelings"

To begin our discussion, let's review what it is that we are talking about in the direct words of some of our Christian sisters who are witnesses to what we are here talking about. They describe "gut feelings" exactly as follows:

- "I would just get an **ache in my chest** or a feeling" (Quote - Lelia Schott)
- "**gut feeling**" (Anonymous testimony from chapter (CH) 10)
- "It just **felt wrong** to me ..." (Anonymous testimony from CH 10)
- "I **did not listen to my heart** ..." (Anonymous testimony from CH 10)
- "but **something just felt wrong**" (Anonymous testimony from CH 10)
- "I have always **felt an almost visceral reaction** ..." (Anonymous testimony from CH 10) (see footnote 89)

I think these testimonies give us a good idea of what we are talking about. We are speaking about something that is internal, it is something inward and it seems to come from a place in the body which is in the gut or in the middle part of the body in some specific way. I think that most of us will find that this general comment makes sense and provides a good description of what we are here talking about.

Addressing the English Translation Problems:
The Next Step to Understanding "Gut Feelings"

An important section of Scripture that has been discussed in this book is one which really is one of the most fundamental texts to this whole issue of maternal intuition linking it to corporal punishment and the inner person. It is found in Jeremiah 17:9:

"The heart is deceitful above all things, and desperately sick; who can understand it?" (Jeremiah 17:9 ESV)

It is in this text that we want to begin this discussion of the major problem of ambiguous English Bible translations.

When we look at Jeremiah 17 in English there is one word in particular which looks very much out of place and does not really seem connected to the subject matter at hand. It is found in v. 10 saying:

I, the LORD, search the heart, I try the reins, even to give every man according to his ways, and according to the fruit of his doings. (King James Version)

In looking at the context of this section of Jeremiah 17, we note that the subject matter is the heart and mind and how God deals with humanity. However, one word is really out of place. It is the word "**reins**."

The word "**reins**" in this passage leads the reader to imagine that God is somehow testing or trying the reins using some kind of zoological description of a comparative nature showing how He tests mankind. But the idea of humanity having "reins", like are used to control or guide a horse or other domesticated animal, just seems out of place. It seems out of place because it is not only out of place, it is a really poor translation of the Hebrew original which is quite clear and easy to understand in this text if it is studied carefully. In modern English parlance, we don't really have another definition for "reins" when we see this word. We think about leather straps or leashes that are used to control the movement of horses or other such animals.

Scholars are aware of this matter and it is their wisdom that helps us understand why the King James Version (which many of the main study concordances and lexicons rely on) uses this word "reins." Let us consider what CBTEL[90] says concerning this issue of "reins."

"Reins, a name for the kidneys, derived from the Latin, *renes*, and in our English Bible employed in those passages of the Old Testament in which the term for kidneys (Hebrew: כליות, *kelayoth*) is used." (Vol. VII, pg.1020)

So, we have a word introduced into the English text which is a type of English transliteration from Latin, which to the English reader today reading the King James Version (or many other versions) in particular is very confusing and, in fact, hides the real meaning of this and several other passages where this word "reins" is retained.

While this word in Hebrew means "kidneys", we must understand that this word is not restricted to meaning solely "kidneys" at all. In no way! What we are going to find is that what this transliterated word from Latin may be hiding is a very important teaching which may also be very relevant to our present inquiry.

First though, let's return to CBTEL for a moment to expand our understanding of this subject. This word in Hebrew, (כליות, *kelayoth*), definitely has a meaning connected directly to the kidneys and to the internal part of an animal in particular which was considered to the best part of a sacrifice, of which there is considerable discussion concerning in the Old Testament.

---

[90] McLintock and Strongs, Cyclopedia of Biblical, Theological and Ecclesiastical Literature: Harper and Brothers, New York, 1883.

"Kidney ... the leaf-fat around which was specially to be a burn-offering, significant of its being the richest and most central part of the victim. (Exodus 29:13,22; Leviticus 3:4.10.15; 4:9; 7:4; 8:16,25; 9:10,19; Isaiah 34:3) (Vol. V, pg.74)

So, *kidney* is indeed an accurate translation of this word. But that is not the only meaning that this word has and here we need further data. Note CBTEL (V, 74.):

"Spoken also of the "reins" of a human being, i.e. the inmost soul, which the ancients supposed to be seated in the **viscera** (compare the Homeric φρην (Greek: *phren*), **mid-riff**, hence mind), both in a physical sense. (Job 16:13; 19:27; Psalm 139:13; Lam. 3:13)"

This definition is further elaborated in the Lexicon commenting on the meaning of the Hebrew word (כליות, *kelayoth*) very beautifully saying:

"figuratively as seat of emotion and affection Job 19:27, Proverbs 19:23; Psalm 16:7; 73:21"[91]

When we understand this, some of these above referenced passages begin to make beautiful sense and start to point us in the direction of an inward reflection towards "gut feelings."

Let us consider some of these passages with more accurate translations taking into consideration this information. What we are going to discover is a whole new level of understanding of these feelings that come from the innermost parts of our being that we often call "gut feelings" or "intuition."

---

[91] New Brown-Driver-Briggs-Gesenius Hebrew English Lexicon, (כלה, kelah, p. 480)

- *"God tests the minds (hearts) and **inner most being**" (*Psa. 7:9 LEB my edits*)*

- *"I will bless Yahweh who advises me; yes, at night my **innermost being** instructs me.⁹²" (*Psalm 16:7 LEB*)*

- *"Prove me, O Yahweh, and test me. Test **my innermost being** and my mind." (*Psalm 26:2 LEB with my own addition*)*

- *"When I became embittered and **my innermost being** was wounded," (*Psalm 73:21 HCSB*)*

- *"You alone created **my inner being**.⁹³ You knitted me together inside my mother." (*Psalm 139:13 GWT*)*

- *"But O Yahweh of hosts, who judges in righteousness, who tests the **inmost being, and the mind**, let me see your retribution upon them, for to you I have revealed my legal case." (*Jeremiah 11:20 LEB*)

- *"Not only do you plant them, they take root. They grow, but also they produce fruit. You are near in their mouths, but far from their **inmost beings**." (*Jer. 12:2 LEB*)

- *"It is I, the Eternal One, who probes the **innermost heart** and examines the **innermost thoughts**. I will compensate each person justly, according to his ways and by what his actions deserve." (*Jeremiah 17:10 VOICE*)

- *"But the Lord of Armies examines the righteous. He sees their **motives and thoughts**." (*Jeremiah 20:12 GWT*)

---

⁹² King David here tells us his innermost being transmits teachings and truths to him from the LORD during the night. It is for this reason that many scholars and commentators have assigned to this word a meaning of "as a seat of emotion or affection." (*ibid.*) When we couple this teaching with Psalm 40:8 also written by King David, we can see that this innermost part of the human being can be a place of knowledge, wisdom and understanding which comes from a divine source.
⁹³ This text is a particularly relevant one for our discussion here because it indicates that this innermost part of the being of the writer, probably the prophet Jeremiah in this Psalm, was something created, formed or fashioned by God. As the texts in this section indicate, this innermost part of human beings has an ability to teach us, so this really represents a very important text for our present inquiry into "gut feelings" and maternal intuition.

These texts are very helpful for our present inquiry because they help to clear up some misunderstanding about the meanings of certain key words and phrases as well as give us a good foundation on which to build our knowledge and understanding of these "gut feelings" or innermost feelings or thoughts of our beings. We find the Bible speaks about them, so it really makes sense for us to pay attention to these texts.

Having said this, it causes the inquiring Bible student to ask: "What about other texts and other Biblical words which also point to what we are referring here to as "gut feelings?" This is a very reasonable and logical question which makes perfect sense in a number of ways. What we are going to find it that there is more knowledge and understanding to be found in God's Word for those willing to seek it out.

The first point is that all of the abovementioned texts were written by men and while certainly men and women both have these internal seats of emotion or affection, it makes sense for us to look at other texts which also refer to the middle part of the anatomy where between males and females, some obvious differences exist.

When we do this, the information one will find further supports our inquiry herein. The first place to start is with another passage from Psalm 40:8:

"I delight to do thy will, O my God: yea, thy law is within my **heart**." (KJV)

When we read this text in the King James Version, we might think on the surface that we are here again encountering the primary Hebrew word for heart (לבב or לב – *lehvahv* or *lehv*). But if we were to assume that, we would be wrong. Psalm 40:8 uses an entirely different Hebrew word (מעים – *meh-geem*) which the King James translators translated by the English word "heart."

133

What is important for our present inquiry though is that when we look at what Psalm 40:8 is teaching, we can see once again that this word in Hebrew has a similar meaning to the Hebrew word 'kidneys' (כליות, *kelayoth*) and that meaning can be once again "**innermost being**" as is the case in Psalm 40:8. What the Psalmist (King David is the sole author of the first 72 Psalms) is telling us is that God's Law penetrates into the most innermost part of our beings due to its importance in our spiritual lives.

Here again it is helpful to quote our Lexicon (see footnote 91) which reinforces this idea of the similarities in meanings among all of these words in Hebrew we are discussing here.

"מעה [which only appears in the Bible in plural - מעים – *meh-geem*] only pl. **internal organs, inward parts (intestines, bowels). belly** ... b. **digestive organs**, but without precision, nearly = **stomach, belly,** ... 2. **Source of procreation** ... 3. **womb,** ... 4. In gen. **inwards, inward part** ... 5. fig. (figurative) **seat of emotions; pity ,,, of God's compassion.**" (*ibid.* pgs. 588-589)

What we are going to find is that once again, we see more evidence for our present inquiry about "gut feelings" in the Bible. While the word "bowels" is the predominant English translation for this Hebrew word, this translation only captures in part the various meanings which the Lexicon makes clear from the various Biblical contexts where this word is used. Let us review several texts in this regard to the above noted Biblical facts.

- *"one who will come forth from **your own body**, he shall be your heir"* (Gen.15:4 NASB)

- *"Upon You have I relied and been sustained from my birth; You are He who took me from **my mother's womb** …* (Psalm 71:6 Amplified Bible)

- *"See how my son who came from **my own body** seeks my life.* (II Sam. 16:11 NKJV)

- *"my heart is like wax; it is melted **inside my body**."* (Psalm 22:14 MEV)

- *""Two nations are in your womb, and two peoples will be separated **from your body**;* (Genesis 25:23 MEV)

- *"Therefore **my inner parts** moan like a lyre for Moab, and **my inmost self**[94] for Kir-hareseth.* (Isaiah 16:11 ESV)

- *"Isn't Ephraim a precious son to me, a delightful child? Whenever I speak against him, I certainly still think about him. Therefore, **my inner being**[95] yearns for him; I will truly have compassion on him. This is the Lord's declaration.* (Jer. 31:20 CSB)

- *"stirring of **your inner parts** and your compassion are held back from me."* (Isaiah 63:15 ESV) – See note below concerning Jeremiah 31:20 because this passage is also speaking about the LORD Himself.

- *"**my innermost being** trembled because of him.* (Song of Songs 5:4 NABRE)

What the evidence indicates is that there is very much a biblical idea of an internal seat of emotion, affection or moral direction which seems very much to be found somewhere in the area of the mid body. This is very much what the ancients

---

[94] This word in Hebrew (קרב – *keh-rev*) is also translated "heart" in some English Old Testament versions and we shall discuss it shortly.

[95] This is also a particularly instructive passage because this is said by the LORD Himself. As human beings are created in His image (Genesis 1:27), both male and female, it makes perfect sense that we would also possess this part of our inner most beings.

believed. There are certainly differences in this regard for men and women, but in general, this idea has a basis in Biblical teachings and more efforts are needed to learn more about it.

To conclude, there is one more Hebrew word, "*keh-rev*" (קרב), which on a number of occasions in the Bible is translated "heart", but has a similar meaning to the words we are here discussing concerning the subject of "gut feelings."

This word has a wide range of meanings linked to the ideas of: "inward part, midst." (*ibid.* pg. 899) It uses this term in a wide range of contexts talking about people and things. For our consideration, however, the most relevant meanings that we wish to focus on once again mean the following:

"2. Of inward part of man; as seat of thought and emotion." (*ibid.* pg. 899)

In addition to this main focus of our line of questioning here, it is important to comment on a number of passages which use this word and speak about women. Note these texts:

- "*Sarah laughed **within herself**, saying, "After I have grown old will I have pleasure, my lord being old also?*" (Genesis 18:12 WEB)
- "*The children struggled together **within her**, and she said, 'If it is thus, why is this happening to me?' So she went to inquire of the Lord.*" (Genesis 25:22 ESV)

To finalize this discussion, it is important to note that many Christian mothers and women have been told that there is nothing good inside of them and not to trust their inner feelings or intuitions. Many of these ideas are based on false teachings and mistaken understandings of the Biblical Revelation. What must be understood is that while humanity is indeed suffering under the pains of sin, there is ample evidence that God does implant His spirit or His spiritual influences inside His children and this matter has a strong relevance to the matter of intuition, especially maternal intuition.

It is very important for a complete and fuller understanding to review some specific passages of Scripture in the context of our discussion at the end here talking about the innermost parts of humanity.

In this regard, our further discussion about the Hebrew word "*keh-rev*" (קרב) is very useful. This is because many passages of Scripture use this word or its cognates to show that God has placed, places or will place spiritual powers or influences that come from Him inside human beings, which must be seen to be positive for humanity. This issue is of particular importance and relevance for our current inquiry concerning maternal intuition because intuitive knowing has a direct spiritual element which is positive and beneficial. Knowing that God is Love (I John 4:8,16) and provides for all of us with a view to positive influences, these texts are ones which I believe we must pay close attention to concerning this subject. Let us review several of them now.

- "*Thus declares the Lord who stretches out the heavens, lays the foundation of the earth, and forms the spirit of man **within him**,*[96] ..." (Zechariah 12:1 NASB)

- "*I will give them a single purpose and put a **new spirit in them**. I will remove their stubborn hearts and give them obedient hearts.*" (Ezekiel 11:19 GWT)

- "*Moreover, I will give you a new heart and **put a new spirit within you** ...*" (Ezekiel 36:26 Amplified Bible)

- "***And I will put my Spirit within you**, and cause you to walk in my statutes and be careful to obey my rules.*" (Ezekiel 36:27 ESV)

---

[96] The first thing to point out is that God is in charge of humanity's spiritual nature, faculties and circumstances. God is the one who makes the spiritual reality of humanity possible.

137

As we see in these texts, God is involved with the formation of the spirit of humanity, in its sustenance and in its future. This is abundantly clear also from numerous New Testament texts. It is only reasonable that when it comes to the matter of maternal intuition or "gut feelings", which seem very much to be spiritual in nature, God through His Spirit seems very much to have an influence in these matters for men and women, but definitely for mothers when it comes to the care and protection of their children in particular.

Conclusion

We can come to some reasonable, studied conclusions concerning this subject of "gut feelings" and their relevance in Biblical teaching. The following points can be noted:

- The Bible describes the innermost beings of humans which have spiritual elements to them.
- Accurate translations of the original Hebrew and Greek words are essential to ensure that we have the opportunity to properly interpret the Biblical texts.
- The ideas of "mind", "innermost being" and "inward parts" are all definite Biblical teachings.
- There is a proven Biblical basis for intuitive feelings or "gut feelings" that originate in the middle part of the body.

For many Christian mothers, who know all too well about the definite reality of these "gut feelings" and having suppressed them or having been told by some religious authorities that these internal leadings or guides, maternal intuition or gut feelings are not positive, I pray this information provides a welcomed relief knowing that our Lord not only understands this issue, but He is the creator, author and sustainer of these holy intuitive feelings, which Christian mothers should cultivate, rely on and feel totally at peace and at home with.

This teaching should be welcomed information for Christian mothers who are contemplating the matter of circumcision and especially if their gut feelings are telling them, "Don't do it!" If you are one of these mothers, listen to your gut feelings knowing they are leading you to the truth of God and you won't suffer being a "regret mother" in the future.

Other books by Samuel Martin

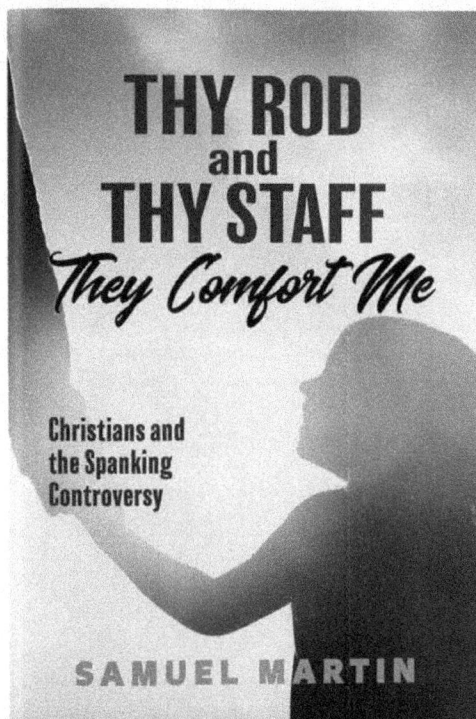

Thy Rod and Thy Staff, They Comfort Me: Christians and the Spanking Controversy – Available free here in soft copy – www.biblechild.com or on Amazon in hard copy – https://www.amazon.com/gp/product/0978533909/ref=dbs_a_def_rwt_bibl_vppi_i1

Reviews of the book

Thy Rod and Thy Staff, They Comfort Me:

Christians and the Spanking Controversy

"I've had a chance to read through your manuscript and I find it very interesting! I think you've made an important contribution, especially to contextualizing biblical ideas about childrearing. I hope you will find a publisher for this book. I'm sure many others would benefit from learning of your research."

Dr. Dawn Devries, John Newton Thomas Professor of Systematic Theology, Union Theological Seminary, USA and contributor to the ground breaking volume "The Child in Christian Thought" (Eerdmans: 2000)

"This is not an easy read, but it is one any Christian who desires to be true to the Bible in the first instance should take time to read. ... In my view this study is a definitive reading of the biblical texts for Christians and non-Christians alike."

Rev. Alistair McBride, Scots Presbyterian Church – Hamilton, New Zealand (see www.repeal59.blogspot.com - July 25 2006)

"Many thanks for sending me a copy of your book. Since I, like so many, cannot read Hebrew, I found your analysis of language fascinating and persuasive. Your exploration of these complex issues is thorough and convincing"

Dr. Philip Greven, Professor Emeritus, Rutgers University, author of "Spare the Child: The Religious Roots of Punishment and the Psychological Impact of Physical Abuse" (Random House, 1992)

"These and other verses, as well as the overall teaching about disciplining children in the Bible is ably discussed by Jerusalem-based Christian biblical scholar Samuel Martin, who has produced a wonderful book, Thy Rod and Thy Staff They Comfort Me: Christians and the Spanking Controversy, available as a free PDF download here with no cost or obligation. Martin has been joined by a significant number of other informed Christian scholars and commentators who are questioning the both the traditional translation and interpretation of these overly quoted verses from the book of Proverbs. I recommend Martin's work for those biblically oriented folk out there who have wondered about what the Bible really says regarding using corporeal punishment of any kind to discipline children—or for that matter anyone who wants to be more informed on this controversial topic."

Professor James D. Tabor, Chair (2004-2014) of the Department of Religious Studies at the University of North Carolina, where he has taught since 1989. He is currently Professor of ancient Judaism and early Christianity.

"I want to take my hat off to Samuel Martin and say, Thanks!

When I think about Samuel Martin, what comes to mind is a contemporary and contextualized, this-world version of William Wilberforce. He certainly has Wilberforce blood running through his veins. He is a Christian living in Jerusalem with an interest in connecting to the rest of the world in ways that are helpful and strategic about how to live out one's faith. Check his website: samuelmartin.blogspot.com. You will find interesting discussions about various biblical subjects.

In addition to being a blogger, Samuel is an author. I just finished reading his book Thy Rod and Thy Staff They Comfort Me: Christians and the Spanking Controversy. I ordered the book from a California source and had it delivered to a Canadian residence http://www.archivescalifornia.com/. Unlike more academic books that I tend to write, which can often be inaccessible to average readers (!), Samuel Martin does a good job of writing with an easy-to-understand touch. For me the greatest benefit in reading his book was to see how a movement towards an anti-spanking position can be developed through Jewish sources and readings of Scripture (as well as Christian ones). He comes to similar conclusions that I do regarding the spanking controversy but his path through the biblical material is quite different - a fascinating read.

Blogger, author and, most importantly, activist! My third thanks to Samuel is that he has reminded me of my own need to be at least to some extent . . . an activist. He has not done this by way of harassment. No, he has shown me this through his own life and example. He would be happy to know that recently I have broken out of my insulated scholarly circles and actually done a handful of radio interviews. Now that is a stretch for a stuffy, old professor of New Testament. Through his own activist work quite extensive as I have watched from afar he is changing the world one person at a time. He does so often by putting people together in ways that help to bring influence on those who perhaps would otherwise not listen. Samuel has reminded me of something that is easily forgotten in the ivory towers of academia, namely, that ideas only work to the degree that there are people willing to influence (other) people about those ideas. So, on three accounts my hat is off to Samuel Martin - blogger, author and activist." - Professor William Webb

Dr. Bill Webb is Adjunct Professor of Biblical Studies at Tyndale Seminary. He has worked as a pastor, chaplain, and professor over a span of over twenty years. In addition to conference speaking ministry, he has published several articles and books, including Returning Home (Sheffield Press, 1993), Slaves, Women, and Homosexuals (IVP, 2001), Discovering Biblical Equality (two chapters; IVP, 2005), Four Views on Moving from the Bible to Theology (one view and responses; Zondervan, 2009), Corporal Punishment in the Bible: A Redemptive Hermeneutic for Troubling Texts (IVP, 2011).

Other books by Samuel Martin

THY ROD and THY STAFF
They Comfort Me BOOK II

14 years in the making, Samuel Martin returns with his second volume in the series, "*Thy Rod and Thy Staff, They Comfort Me*," further strenthening an already compelling case against corporal punishment in this new book, focused on the New Testament book of Hebrews chapter 12:5-11, which is a key text quoted by many Christians today in their belief in corporal punishment.

FEATURES OF THIS NEW BOOK ARE:
- The original manuscript order of Hebrews and its importance?
- Who wrote Hebrews and why that is important?
- If Paul wrote Hebrews, why did he not identify himself openly?
- What geographical region was Hebrews written to?
- When was the book of Hebrews written?
- What is the main subject of the book of Hebrews?
- Who is the book of Hebrews relevant for today?
- How does this survey of Hebrews link to our understanding of the debate concerning spanking children in the 21st century?

The first book in the series, '*Thy Rod and Thy Staff, They Comfort Me: Christians and the Spanking Controversy*,' (published in 2006) was not sold, but has been available as a free download on numerous sites on the web and through www.biblechild.com. A printed version is now also available for purchase through Amazon.

THY ROD and THY STAFF
They Comfort Me
BOOK II

The Book of Hebrews and the Corporal Punishment of Children in the Christian Context

SAMUEL MARTIN

Thy Rod and Thy Staff, They Comfort Me: Book II – The Book of Hebrews and the Corporal Punishment of Children in the Christian Context – Available on Amazon in hard copy.

https://www.amazon.com/Samuel-Martin/e/B00HP94ZZA/ref=dp_byline_cont_pop_book_1

Reviews of the book

Thy Rod and Thy Staff, They Comfort Me: Book II

The Book of Hebrews and the Corporal

Punishment of Children in the Christian Context

"Samuel Martin does a good job of writing with an easy-to-understand touch ... He comes to similar conclusions that I do regarding the spanking controversy."

- Professor William Webb, Adjunct Professor of Biblical Studies, Tyndale Seminary, Canada and author of the book "Corporal Punishment in the Bible: A Redemptive Movement Hermeneutic for Troubling Texts" (InterVarsity, 2011)

"I think you present a well-crafted argument."

Pastor Crystal Lutton, author of "Biblical Parenting"

"a very provocative and stimulating perspective of Hebrews."

Clay Clarkson, author of "Heartfelt Discipline: Following God's Path of Life to the Heart of Your Child."

Other books by Samuel Martin

THY ROD and THY STAFF
They Comfort Me BOOK III

10 years in the making, Samuel Martin returns with his third volume in the series, "Thy Rod and Thy Staff, They Comfort Me," responding to an urgent need in Christ's Body to address the falsehoods Christian mothers have been told with regard to their God-given maternal intuition.

Christian mothers have been told:

- You are flawed
- You are dirty and need to be cleaned up
- Your heart is full of evil and needs to be ignored and suppressed
- There is nothing good inside you
- Yuo cannot trust yourself and your God-given intuition and maternal leadings
- you are "too sensitive" and that is bad
- What you think you "just know" is wrong and almost certainly not from God
- Do not ever trust your feelings. They are wrong and against God. If you listen to your own feelings, you will be embracing evil

This book seeks to support Christian mothers as they reconnect with their holy, God-given intuition to help them feel at peace in their body, heart, and soul.

"Samuel Martin does a good job of writing with an easy-to-understand touch...He comes to similar conclusions that I do regarding the spanking controversy."
- Professor William Webb, Adjunct Professor of Biblical Studies, Tyndale Seminary, Canada, and author of *Corporal Punishment in the Bible: A Redemptive-Movement Hermeneutic for Troubling Texts* (InterVarsity, 2011)

"I think you present a well-crafted argument."
- Pastor Crystal Lutton, author of *Biblical Parenting*

"...a very provocative and stimulating perspective of Hebrews."
- Clay Clarkson, author of *Heartfelt Discipline: Following God's Path of Life to the Heart of Your Child*

The first books in the series, "Thy Rod and Thy Staff, They Comfort Me" series.

THY ROD and THY STAFF *They Comfort Me* BOOK III

THY ROD and THY STAFF *They Comfort Me*

A Biblical Study on Maternal Intuition and its link to the Issue of Spanking Children

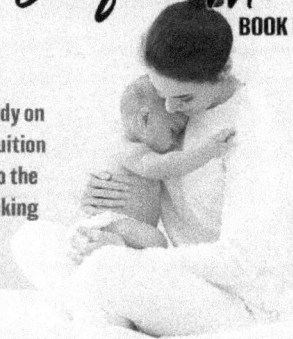

SAMUEL MARTIN

Thy Rod and Thy Staff, They Comfort Me: Book III – A Biblical Study on Maternal Intuition and its link to the Issue of Spanking Children – Available on Amazon in hard copy and e-book formats.

https://www.amazon.com/Samuel-Martin/e/B00HP94ZZA/ref=dp_byline_cont_pop_book_1

Reviews of the book

Thy Rod and Thy Staff, They Comfort Me: Book III

A Biblical Study on Maternal Intuition and its link

to the Issue of Spanking Children

"Samuel Martin has been so helpful - breaking down scripture and historical context as it applies to living and mothering today, so in spite of my biases, I picked up this next book from him.

The reason for this book is the reason I was hesitant. I, too, was raised to never trust my own intuition or instincts. Having read this book, I see now how flawed that teaching is. Does Christ not redeem the whole person?

For me, this book has been very affirming and healing. Ignoring my intuition as "always flawed" has landed me in some very dangerous situations. I wish I had read this long ago. But I'm grateful for it now.

Not only for this affirmation and deeper understanding of what scripture says, but also for being built up spiritually - maturing and being able to parse the teaching of men from the teaching of scripture." — Christina Dronen, https://gentlechristianparenting.com/

"Samuel Martin's first Thy Rod and thy Staff book was the first gentle parenting book I read and it was like a breath of fresh air. I've always felt like there was something wrong with so many Christians using scriptures to say that the Bible tells us to spank. When I came across that book everything made so much sense. Samuel Martin is very thorough and explains things from a biblical perspective in great detail. This book has been a huge blessing as well and it has made me feel more confident in following those God given instincts as a wife and mother. May God bless the Author and may God bless others with the teachings in this book!" — Debbie Donisa, Amazon Review

Other books by Samuel Martin

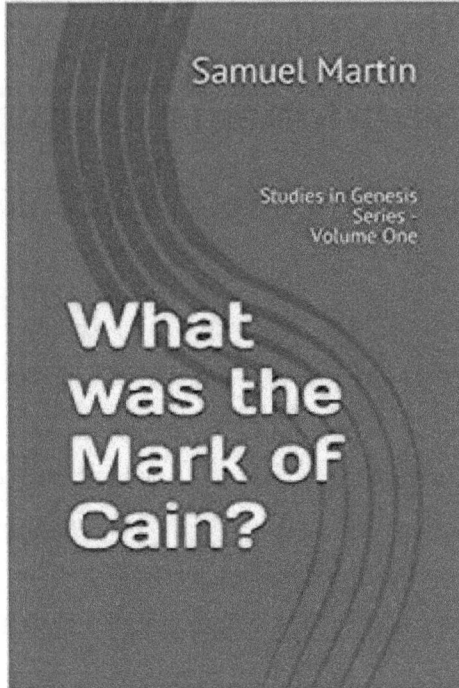

What was the Mark of Cain? Scholars and lay people alike have been asking this question for centuries. In this new book, Samuel Martin proposes a new idea to help answer this age-old question. This new book stresses the following points in seeking to identify what was the Mark of Cain:

- ✓ The early narratives in Genesis cannot be understood properly without an appreciation of the fact that these narratives have very strong symbolic teachings associated with them relating to the Holy Temple
- ✓ Solid comparative studies of the specific texts in Genesis relating to this story with other Biblical passages will pay great dividends in helping to understand what the Mark of Cain was
- ✓ In this book, we propose a number of interesting and thought provoking suggestions about Cain and Abel age's at the time when Abel died
- ✓ A new proposal concerning the Biblical translation of the "Land of Nod."

This book is available on Amazon at the following link:

www.amazon.com/Samuel-Martin/e/B00HP94ZZA/ref=dp_byline_cont_pop_book_1

Other books by Samuel Martin

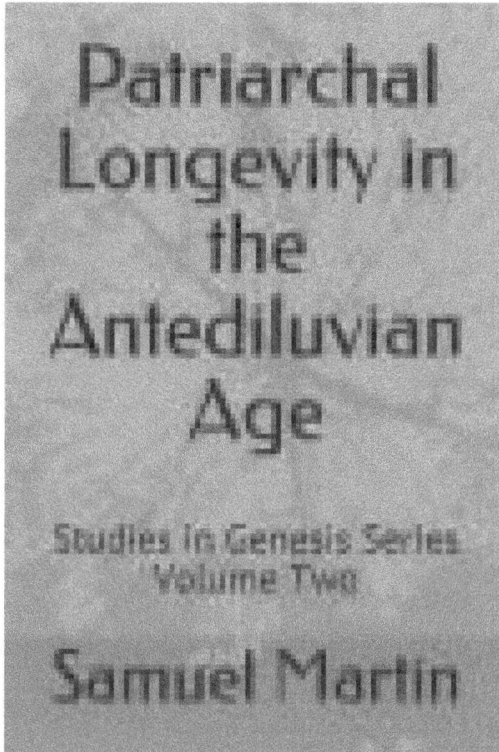

Patriarchal Longevity in the Antediluvian Age

Studies In Genesis Series
Volume Two

Samuel Martin

One of the most interesting aspects to the early history of human kind concerns the Biblical data showing that certain individuals are identified as having lived lives reaching up to almost 1,000 years of age. We today look at these Biblical texts and wonder if they are true or if they just represent ancient myths that primitive mankind believed in.

In this new publication, we are going to explore this question with a view to illuminating difficult passages of the Holy Scripture. We believe that the LORD has given us all the information that we need within the Scriptures themselves to answer all the questions that we may have on most subjects. Understanding how the Patriarchs in the Antediluvian Age lived to be so old is no exception.

https://www.amazon.com/Samuel-Martin/e/B00HP94ZZA/ref=dp_byline_cont_pop_book_1

Testimonies from Christian moms about the book Thy Rod and Thy Staff, They Comfort Me: Christians and the Spanking Controversy

"Wow! I'm so glad that you have been able to give this book out to so many. [over 400 in the last 12 months] I still am so grateful that I discovered it. It has helped us to parent each of our children with love and respect. We have recently become foster parents and I was so proud to be able to say that we were Christians who don't spank. They make foster parents sign a contract to not spank foster children if they use corporal punishment with their own children. They are so used to Christians spanking there own children and seemed surprised that we didn't. Blessing to you and all the work that you do."

"I would very much appreciate a PDF copy of your book "Thy Rod and Thy Staff, They Comfort Me; Christians and the Spanking Controversy".

"Well since then I married and brought up two daughters. In the [mentions denomination] culture of the time, under pressure from the ministry, I did apply a limited amount of spanking with my elder daughter for a very few years, but by the time my second daughter was born I had come to the view that this was not a Christian way to bring up a child, and neither daughter was spanked from then on.

My daughters are now two fine, loving adult ladies. My eldest daughter is now married, and has a two-year-old son, and a three-week-old daughter.

She too is now concerned to bring up her children in a correct way, but is also aware of some pressure on her to apply spanking, which she has thus far resisted."

"Hello, I am a Christian, expecting my first child in August. I am floored by the willingness of many Christians to twist the Word of God so horribly. I look forward to having this book as a tool to back up what I already believe about parenting with the grace God parents us."

"I am a new mom to a beautiful baby girl and have recently found your blog! I was hoping to get a copy of your book, Thy Rod and Thy Staff, They Comfort Me. I was spanked as a child and always thought that was what God wanted but THANK JESUS for the many revelations I have had recently about parenting! I just feel so genuinely excited about raising my daughter now...thinking God expected/wanted me to hit my kids to teach them right always felt wrong to me but I was prepared to do it because I really believed that to be what God wanted. I'm so grateful my eyes have been opened. And so looking forward to educating myself more on this issue. Thank you for what you do!!! You are a blessing."

"Hello! I am so excited about your book. The biblical spanking issue is one I feel God has put on my heart since childhood, as I was spanked and have vivid memories of it. Where many have forgotten the child's perspective with spankings, I remember them well and with much pain."

"I'd love to read a copy of your book. My husband and I were both abused and while we choose not to spank, we have hit our children in anger in the past. As we have worked on our abuse issues and grown closer to God, it has gotten easier to take a moment and not react out of anger.

Our children's guidance counselor gave a class on Love and Logic and that also really helped.

One of my friends shared your status on Facebook today. I shared it after reading the discussion left in the comments of that status. I thought you'd be interested in what I posted:

This is great. I think it's pretty sad that people are using this status to argue that hitting a child is necessary. How else do you discipline? Consequences, removal, distraction...all depending on the situation and age of the child.

We get disciplined at work and in society without hitting. In fact, we're told hitting and bullying is wrong. Yet we think kids are too stupid to learn without hitting...while being smart enough to understand that hitting from a caregiver is different?"

"I am in full support and am still so extremely thankful for your book. It has given me such resolve and a sense of peace in what I am doing with my daughter. I am indeed treading in new water, as far as my own family is concerned, but I'm also blazing a path to be seen, and hopefully, someday emulated by fellow family, as I go. My family will be the evidence that it can be done by someone with little experience in gentle rearing, but a determination given and confirmed by God Himself. I want to thank you so much for your work. I plan on passing it on to anyone who will listen."

"Yes, thanks. I was tremendously blessed [by your book]. I even went through it with my Pastor, who of course, is old school and is moderately pro-spanking, like most Christians. It challenged him, but did not convince him completely. It's really hard to get through to people who are so ingrained to spanking. But it did make him think and question many things, so I'm going to continue to work on him, and hopefully the Holy Spirit will enlighten him.

It's amazing to see what a strong hold "tradition" has on people because exegetically and logically, I don't see the proof for spanking. My Pastor was even a little taken back because he couldn't find exegeses from any of his commentaries on the "spanking" passages. It seems like it's just been taken for granted over all these years. Thanks for you all your hard work!"

About the Author

Samuel Martin was born in England and is the youngest child of Dr. Ernest L. and Helen R. Martin, who are both Americans and natives of the state of Oklahoma.

He lived in the UK for the first seven years of his life before moving to the USA with his family. He lived in the USA until 2001 when he married a native Israeli Christian and relocated to live in Jerusalem, where he currently resides. He and his wife have two girls.

His experience with biblical scholarship began at an early age. His father lead a program in conjunction with Hebrew University and the late Professor Benjamin Mazar, where over a five year period, some 450 college students came to work on an archaeological excavation in Jerusalem starting in 1969.

Since that first trip, Samuel has visited Israel on 14 different occasions living more than 19 years of his life in the country. He has toured all areas of Israel as well as worked in several archaeological excavations.

He writes regularly on biblical subjects with a particular interest in children, families, nature, science, the Bible, and gender in the Biblical context. He holds an MA from the University of the Holy Land in Inter-Cultural Studies and the Bible.

Website: www.biblechild.com
Contact: info@biblechild.com
Facebook: https://www.facebook.com/byblechyld/
Blog: www.samuelmartin.blogspot.com
Amazon: https://www.amazon.com/Samuel-Martin/e/B00HP94ZZA/ref=dp_byline_cont_book_1